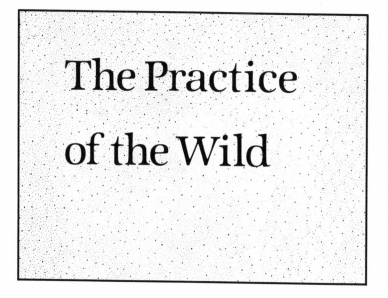

The Practice

of the Wild

Essays by

Gary Snyder

North Point Press
San Francisco 1990

The author and publisher wish to gratefully acknowledge
the following publications in which parts of this book first
appeared: *Sierra*, *CoEvolution Quarterly*, *Witness*, New
Directions, and *Antaeus*. "Good, Wild, Sacred" was also
previously published in a chapbook by Five Seasons Press in
Great Britain.

LIBRARY OF CONGRESS CATALOGING-IN-PUBLICATION DATA
Snyder, Gary.
    The practice of the wild   :   essays / by Gary Snyder.
      p.   cm.
    ISBN 0-86547-453-2. — ISBN 0-86547-454-0 (pbk.)
    I. Title.
PS3569.N88P7   1990   90-7590
814'.54—dc20

North Point Press
850 Talbot Avenue
Berkeley, California
94706

This book is for Carole

on the trail

Contents

By Way of Thanks

Most of the essays in this book had their inception in talks, workshops, and conversations that took place over the last fifteen years. I owe much to the many fine people and places that called these thoughts forth. Although my work and curiosity take me far afield, I am foremost a person of the Yuba River country in the Sierra Nevada of northern California. The San Juan Ridge and the many people there with whom I share work, rituals, and ideas are at the core of this exercise. First I want to thank the person to whom this book is dedicated, my wife and partner Carole Koda, who read and discussed it all while in progress. Jerry Tecklin, Bob Greensfelder, Jean Greensfelder, Jim Pyle, Pat Ferris, Gen Snyder, Kai Snyder, Chuck Dockham, Bruce Boyd, Holly Tornheim, Steve Beckwitt, Eric Beckwitt, David Tecklin, Steve Sanfield, Lennie Brackett, Don Harkin, Michael Killigrew, Robin Martin, Arlo Acton, Tony Mociun, David Samuels, Nelson Foster, Masa Uehara, Paul Noel, DeOnne Noel, Will Staple, Michael Brackney, Bob Erickson, Moth Lorenzon, Robbie Thompson, Ann Greensfelder, Sara Greensfelder, and Jacquie Bellon have all given me particular (often nonverbal) pointers. The whole San Juan Ridge community has been teacher and friend.

I have learned much from my many trips to Alaska. Gary Holthaus of the Alaska Humanities Forum taught me where to go and shared his deep appreciation of the north with me at community gatherings in places as diverse as Aleknagik, Fort Yukon, Juneau, Homer, Sitka, and Bethel. Steve Grubis led me down the Kobuk

River and Bonnie and Hans Boenish put us up. Ron and Suzie Scollon introduced me to their work in Athapaskan and other northern language groups, and to the snowy mountains north of Haines. Dick Dauenhauer and Nora Marks Dauenhauer showed me a little of the southeast Alaskan cultural milieu. Jim Kari introduced me to the subtleties of place names. Dick Nelson led me over muskeg and surf into pathless wilds. I thank Roger Rom for teaming up with the University of Alaska to sponsor two successive summer field trips we led in the Brooks Range and James Katz for putting together a floating seminar on the Tatshenshini River. Jan Straley had us chasing Humpback Whales' flukes (as part of her research) in Icy Straits, and Jonathan White sailed the *Crusader* right through Ford's Terror just to look at a yosemite full of ice and water.

Many of my colleagues at the University of California at Davis share the interest in wildness and the interaction of nature and culture. I have especially appreciated the insights of David Robertson, Jack Hicks, Will Baker, Scott McLean, and David Scofield Wilson. Students in my lectures and seminars have tested my notions and opened my outlook with their fresh and perceptive views. Several small but timely University Research Grants, and the friendly and interested cooperation of the faculty and staff of the English Department, all helped.

Some of these essays first took form as talks given at the San Francisco Jung Institute (several as stimulating collaborations with James Hillman, Gioia Timpanelli, and Ursula Le Guin). I also gave sections of this book as talks at the Teton Science School in Jackson Hole, at Lindisfarne Association gatherings, at the Schumacher Society's annual meeting in Bristol, England, at the Wilderness Conference of 1984 sponsored by the University of Montana, at the Hudson Valley Watershed Conference, at Hollyhock Farm in British Columbia, and many other places. John Stokes (and the Australian Arts Council) made it possible for Nanao Sakaki and me to travel extensively in Australia and visit parts of the central desert that are not usually open to visitors.

Many friends read and offered sound advice on all or parts of the work-in-progress. David Padwa and Peter Coyote gave me bold and useful encouragement, as did Jim Dodge and Peter Berg. Max Oelschlager and Wendell Berry made keen suggestions.

Nanao Sakaki of Japan and Turtle Island, Lee Swenson, George Sessions, Tom Lyon of Utah and the Rockies, Paul Shepard, Drum Hadley of Guadalupe Canyon Ranch, Dave Foreman of Earth First!, Dolores La Chappelle, Sherman Paul, Malcolm Margolin, Bob Uhl of Kotzebue, Alaska, Jerry Martien of Arcata, Kurt Hoelting of Petersburg, Alaska, Jerry Gorsline of Port Townsend, Fraser and Ali Lang of Bridge River, British Columbia, Kelly Kindscher of Kansas, Gary Lawless of Maine, Dale Pendell now of Santa Cruz, Greg Keeler of Bozeman, Allen Ginsberg of New York and Boulder, Jack Turner of the Tetons, Jack Loeffler of Santa Fe, Jim Snyder of Yosemite, Ed Grumbine, Jaan Kaplinski of Estonia, Julia Martin of Capetown, South Africa, John Seed of New South Wales, Sansei Yamao of Yakushima, Japan, Peter Bluecloud of Akwesasne, Paul Winter, Lewis MacAdams of The Friends of the L.A. River, Non and Bird of the mountains near Trinidad, Colorado, Dan Kozlowsky of Wisconsin, Clayton Eshleman of *Sulfur*, Michael McClure of the Class Mammalia, and Morinaga Sōko Roshi of Daishū-in are a few among the many remarkable friends whose lives and works have been part of my meditations as I put together this text.

I am grateful to Catherine McClellan, professor emerita of anthropology at the University of Wisconsin, for permission to retell the version of "The Woman Who Married a Bear" that she heard from Maria Johns in the early years of her career, as well as her memories of Maria Johns.

I thank Gary Capshaw for the gift of the desk and his memories of Lew Welch. I especially want to thank Yvon and Malinda Chouinard and the Patagonia Corporation for generous and swiftly expedited financial help in the final year of writing.

With so many good friends and critics it would seem hard to believe that there might still be errors or infelicities. Whatever they are, they belong entirely to me.

The Practice
of the Wild

The Etiquette
of Freedom

The Compact

One June afternoon in the early seventies I walked through the crackly gold grasses to a neat but unpainted cabin at the back end of a ranch near the drainage of the South Yuba in northern California. It had no glass in the windows, no door. It was shaded by a huge Black Oak. The house looked abandoned and my friend, a student of native California literature and languages, walked right in. Off to the side, at a bare wooden table, with a mug of coffee, sat a solid old gray-haired Indian man. He acknowledged us, greeted my friend, and gravely offered us instant coffee and canned milk. He was fine, he said, but he would never go back to a VA hospital again. From now on if he got sick he would stay where he was. He liked being home. We spoke for some time of people and places along the western slope of the northern Sierra Nevada, the territories of Concow and Nisenan people. Finally my friend broke his good news: "Louie, I have found another person who speaks Nisenan." There were perhaps no more than three people alive speaking Nisenan at that time, and Louie was one of them. "Who?" Louie asked. He told her name. "She lives back of Oroville. I can bring her here, and you two can speak." "I know her from way back," Louie said. "She wouldn't want to come over here. I don't think I should see her. Besides, her family and mine never did get along."

That took my breath away. Here was a man who would not let the mere threat of cultural extinction stand in the way of his (and her) values. To well-meaning sympathetic white people this response is almost incomprehensible. In the world of his people, never overpopulated, rich in acorn, deer, salmon, and flicker feathers, to cleave to such purity, to be perfectionists about matters of family or clan, were affordable luxuries. Louie and his fellow Nisenan had more important business with each other than conversations. I think he saw it as a matter of keeping their dignity, their pride, and their own ways—regardless of what straits they had fallen upon—until the end.

Coyote and Ground Squirrel do not break the compact they have with each other that one must play predator and the other play game. In the wild a baby Black-tailed Hare gets maybe one free chance to run across a meadow without looking up. There won't be a second. The sharper the knife, the cleaner the line of the carving. We can appreciate the elegance of the forces that shape life and the world, that have shaped every line of our bodies—teeth and nails, nipples and eyebrows. We also see that we must try to live without causing unnecessary harm, not just to fellow humans but to all beings. We must try not to be stingy, or to exploit others. There will be enough pain in the world as it is.

Such are the lessons of the wild. The school where these lessons can be learned, the realms of caribou and elk, elephant and rhinoceros, orca and walrus, are shrinking day by day. Creatures who have traveled with us through the ages are now apparently doomed, as their habitat—and the old, old habitat of humans—falls before the slow-motion explosion of expanding world economies. If the lad or lass is among us who knows where the secret heart of this Growth-Monster is hidden, let them please tell us where to shoot the arrow that will slow it down. And if the secret heart stays secret and our work is made no easier, I for one will keep working for wildness day by day.

"Wild and free." An American dream-phrase loosing images: a long-maned stallion racing across the grasslands, a V of Canada Geese high and honking, a squirrel chattering and leaping limb to limb overhead in an oak. It also sounds like an ad for a Harley-Davidson. Both words, profoundly political and sensitive as they are, have become consumer baubles. I hope to investigate the meaning of *wild* and how it connects with *free* and what one would want to do with these meanings. To be truly free one must take on the basic conditions as they are—painful, impermanent, open, imperfect—and then be grateful for impermanence and the freedom it grants us. For in a fixed universe there would be no freedom. With that freedom we improve the campsite, teach children, oust tyrants. The world is nature, and in the long run inevitably wild, because the wild, as the process and essence of nature, is also an ordering of impermanence.

Although *nature* is a term that is not of itself threatening, the idea of the "wild" in civilized societies—both European and Asian—is often associated with unruliness, disorder, and violence. The Chinese word for nature, *zi-ran* (Japanese *shizen*) means "self-thus." It is a bland and general word. The word for wild in Chinese, *ye* (Japanese *ya*), which basically means "open country," has a wide set of meanings: in various combinations the term becomes illicit connection, desert country, an illegitimate child (open-country child), prostitute (open-country flower), and such. In an interesting case, *ye-man zi-yu* ("open-country southern-tribal-person-freedom") means "wild license." In another context "open-country story" becomes "fiction and fictitious romance." Other associations are usually with the rustic and uncouth. In a way *ye* is taken to mean "nature at its worst." Although the Chinese and Japanese have long given lip service to nature, only the early Daoists might have thought that wisdom could come of wildness.

Thoreau says "give me a wildness no civilization can endure." That's clearly not difficult to find. It is harder to imagine a civilization that wildness can endure, yet this is just what we must try to do. Wildness is not just the "preservation of the world," it *is* the world. Civilizations east and west have long been on a collision course with wild nature, and now the developed nations in particular have the witless power to destroy not only individual creatures but whole species, whole processes, of the earth. We need a civilization that can live fully and creatively together with wildness. We must start growing it right here, in the New World.

When we think of wilderness in America today, we think of remote and perhaps designated regions that are commonly alpine, desert, or swamp. Just a few centuries ago, when virtually *all* was wild in North America, wilderness was not something exceptionally severe. Pronghorn and bison trailed through the grasslands, creeks ran full of salmon, there were acres of clams, and grizzlies, cougar, and bighorn sheep were common in the lowlands. There were human beings, too: North America was *all populated*. One might say yes, but thinly—which raises the question of according to whom. The fact is, people were everywhere. When the Spanish foot soldier Alvar Núñez Cabeza de Vaca and his two companions (one of whom was African) were wrecked on the beach of what is now Galveston, and walked to the Rio Grande valley and then south back into Mexico between 1528 and 1536, there were few times in the whole eight years that they were not staying at a native settlement or camp. They were always on trails.

It has always been part of basic human experience to live in a culture of wilderness. There has been no wilderness without some kind of human presence for several hundred thousand years. Nature is not a place to visit, it is *home*—and within that home territory there are more familiar and less familiar places. Often there are areas that are difficult and remote, but all are *known* and even named. One August I was at a pass in the Brooks Range of northern Alaska at the headwaters of the Koyukuk River, a green three-thousand-foot tundra pass between the broad ranges, open and gentle, dividing the waters that flow to the Arctic Sea from the Yukon. It is as remote a place as you could be in North America, no roads, and the trails are those made by migrating caribou. Yet this pass has been steadily used by Inupiaq people of the north slope and Athapaskan people of the Yukon as a regular north-south trade route for at least seven thousand years.

All of the hills and lakes of Alaska have been named in one or another of the dozen or so languages spoken by the native people, as the researches of Jim Kari (1982; 1985) and others have shown. Euro-American mapmakers name these places after transient exploiters, or their own girlfriends, or home towns in the Lower 48. The point is: it's all in the native story, yet only the tiniest trace of human presence through all that time shows. The place-based stories the people tell, and the naming they've done, is their archaeology, architecture, and *title* to the land. Talk about living lightly.

Cultures of wilderness live by the life and death lessons of subsistence economies. But what can we now mean by the words *wild* and for that matter *nature*? Languages meander like great rivers leaving oxbow traces over forgotten beds, to be seen only from the air or by scholars. Language is like some kind of infinitely interfertile family of species spreading or mysteriously declining over time, shamelessly and endlessly hybridizing, changing its own rules as it goes.

Words are used as signs, as stand-ins, arbitrary and temporary, even as language reflects (and informs) the shifting values of the peoples whose minds it inhabits and glides through. We have faith in "meaning" the way we might believe in wolverines—putting trust in the occasional reports of others or on the authority of once seeing a pelt. But it is sometimes worth tracking these tricksters back.

The Words Nature, Wild, and Wilderness

Take *nature* first. The word *nature* is from Latin *natura*, "birth, constitution, character, course of things"—ultimately from *nasci*, to be born. So we have *nation, natal, native, pregnant*. The probable Indo-European root (via Greek *gna*—hence cognate, agnate) is *gen* (Sanskrit *jan*), which provides *generate* and *genus*, as well as *kin* and *kind*.

The word gets two slightly different meanings. One is "the outdoors"—the physical world, including all living things. Nature by this definition is a norm of the world that is apart from the features or products of civilization and human will. The machine, the artifact, the devised, or the extraordinary (like a two-headed calf) is spoken of as "unnatural." The other meaning, which is broader, is "the material world or its collective objects and phenomena," including the products of human action and intention. As an agency nature is defined as "the creative and regulative physical power which is conceived of as operating in the material world and as the immediate cause of all its phenomena." Science and some sorts of mysticism rightly propose that *everything* is natural. By these lights there is nothing unnatural about New York City, or toxic wastes, or atomic energy, and nothing—by definition—that we do or experience in life is "unnatural."

(The "supernatural"? One way to deal with it is to say that "the supernatural" is a name for phenomena which are reported by so few people as to leave their reality in doubt. Nonetheless these events— ghosts, gods, magical transformations, and such—are described often enough to make them continue to be intriguing and, for some, credible.)

The physical universe and all its properties—I would prefer to use the word *nature* in this sense. But it will come up meaning "the outdoors" or "other-than-human" sometimes even here.

The word *wild* is like a gray fox trotting off through the forest, ducking behind bushes, going in and out of sight. Up close, first glance, it is "wild"—then farther into the woods next glance it's "wyld" and it recedes via Old Norse *villr* and Old Teutonic *wilthijaz* into a faint pre-Teutonic *ghweltijos* which means, still, wild and maybe wooded (*wald*) and lurks back there with possible connections to *will*, to Latin *silva* (forest, sauvage), and to the Indo-European root *ghwer*, base of Latin *ferus* (feral, fierce), which swings us around to Thoreau's "awful ferity" shared by virtuous people and lovers. The Oxford English Dictionary has it this way:

Of animals—not tame, undomesticated, unruly.

Of plants—not cultivated.

Of land—uninhabited, uncultivated.

Of foodcrops—produced or yielded without cultivation.

Of societies—uncivilized, rude, resisting constituted government.

Of individuals—unrestrained, insubordinate, licentious, dissolute, loose. "Wild and wanton widowes"—1614.

Of behavior—violent, destructive, cruel, unruly.

Of behavior—artless, free, spontaneous. "Warble his native wood-notes wild"—John Milton.

Wild is largely defined in our dictionaries by what—from a human standpoint—it is not. It cannot be seen by this approach for what it *is*. Turn it the other way:

Of animals—free agents, each with its own endowments, living within natural systems.

Of plants—self-propagating, self-maintaining, flourishing in accord with innate qualities.

Of land—a place where the original and potential vegetation and fauna are intact and in full interaction and the landforms are entirely the result of nonhuman forces. Pristine.

Of foodcrops—food supplies made available and sustainable by the natural excess and exuberance of wild plants in their growth and in the production of quantities of fruit or seeds.

Of societies—societies whose order has grown from within and is maintained by the force of consensus and custom rather than explicit legislation. Primary cultures, which consider themselves the original and eternal inhabitants of their territory. Societies which resist economic and political domination by civilization. Societies whose economic system is in a close and sustainable relation to the local ecosystem.

Of individuals—following local custom, style, and etiquette without concern for the standards of the metropolis or nearest trading post. Unintimidated, self-reliant, independent. "Proud and free."

Of behavior—fiercely resisting any oppression, confinement, or exploitation. Far-out, outrageous, "bad," admirable.

Of behavior—artless, free, spontaneous, unconditioned. Expressive, physical, openly sexual, ecstatic.

Most of the senses in this second set of definitions come very close to being how the Chinese define the term *Dao*, the *way* of Great Nature: eluding analysis, beyond categories, self-organizing, self-informing, playful, surprising, impermanent, insubstantial, independent, complete, orderly, unmediated, freely manifesting, self-authenticating, self-willed, complex, quite simple. Both empty and real at the same time. In some cases we might call it sacred. It is not far from the Buddhist term *Dharma* with its original senses of forming and firming.

The word *wilderness*, earlier *wyldernesse*, Old English *wildeornes*, possibly from "wild-deer-ness" (*deor*, deer and other forest animals) but more likely "wildern-ness," has the meanings:

A large area of wild land, with original vegetation and wildlife, ranging from dense jungle or rainforest to arctic or alpine "white wilderness."

A wasteland, as an area unused or useless for agriculture or pasture.

A space of sea or air, as in Shakespeare, "I stand as one upon a Rock, environ'd with a Wilderness of Sea" (*Titus Andronicus*). The oceans.

A place of danger and difficulty: where you take your own chances, depend on your own skills, and do not count on rescue.

This world as contrasted with heaven. "I walked through the wildernesse of this world" (*Pilgrim's Progress*).

A place of abundance, as in John Milton, "a wildernesse of sweets."

Milton's usage of wilderness catches the very real condition of energy and richness that is so often found in wild systems. "A wildernesse of sweets" is like the billions of herring or mackerel babies in the ocean, the cubic miles of krill, wild prairie grass seed (leading to the bread of this day, made from the germs of grasses)—all the incredible fecundity of small animals and plants, feeding the web. But from another side, wilderness has implied chaos, eros, the unknown, realms of taboo, the habitat of both the ecstatic and the demonic. In both senses it is a place of archetypal power, teaching, and challenge.

Wildness

So we can say that New York City and Tokyo are "natural" but not "wild." They do not deviate from the laws of nature, but they are habitat so exclusive in the matter of who and what they give shelter to, and so intolerant of other creatures, as to be truly odd. Wilderness is a *place* where the wild potential is fully expressed, a diversity of living and nonliving beings flourishing according to their own sorts of order. In ecology we speak of "wild systems." When an ecosystem is fully functioning, all the members are present at the assembly. To speak of wilderness is to speak of wholeness. Human beings came out of that wholeness, and to consider the possibility of reactivating membership in the Assembly of All Beings is in no way regressive.

By the sixteenth century the lands of the Occident, the countries of Asia, and all the civilizations and cities from the Indian subcontinent to the coast of North Africa were becoming ecologically impoverished. The people were rapidly becoming nature-illiterate. Much of the original vegetation had been destroyed by the expansion of grazing or agriculture, and the remaining land was of no great human economic use, "waste," mountain regions and deserts. The lingering larger animals—big cats, desert sheep, serows, and such— managed to survive by retreating to the harsher habitats. The leaders of these civilizations grew up with less and less personal knowledge of animal behavior and were no longer taught the intimate wide-ranging plant knowledge that had once been universal. By way of tradeoff they learned "human management," administration, rhetorical skills. Only the most marginal of the *paysan*, people of the land, kept up practical plant and animal lore and memories of the old ways. People who grew up in towns or cities, or on large estates, had less chance to learn how wild systems work. Then major blocks of citified mythology (Medieval Christianity and then the "Rise of Science") denied first soul, then consciousness, and finally even sentience to the natural world. Huge numbers of Europeans, in the climate of a nature-denying mechanistic ideology, were losing the opportunity for direct experience of nature.

A new sort of nature-traveler came into existence: men who went out as resource scouts, financed by companies or aristocratic families, penetrating the lightly populated lands of people who lived in and with the wilderness. Conquistadores and priests. Europe had killed off the wolves and bears, deforested vast areas, and overgrazed the hills. The search for slaves, fish, sugar, and precious metals ran over the edge of the horizon and into Asia, Africa, and the New World. These overrefined and warlike states once more came up against wild nature and natural societies: people who lived without Church or State. In return for gold or raw sugar, the white men had to give up something of themselves: they had to look into their own sense of what it meant to be a human being, wonder about the nature of hierarchy, ask if life was worth the honor of a king, or worth gold. (A lost and starving man stands and examines the nicked edge of his sword and his frayed Spanish cape in a Florida swamp.)

Some, like Nuño de Guzmán, became crazed and sadistic. "When he began to govern this province, it contained 25,000 Indians, subjugated and peaceful. Of these he has sold 10,000 as slaves, and the others, fearing the same fate, have abandoned their villages" (Todorov, 1985, 134). Cortés, the conqueror of Mexico, ended up a beaten, depressed beggar-to-the-throne. Alvar Núñez, who for eight years walked naked across Texas and New Mexico, came out transformed into a person of the New World. He had rejoined the old ways and was never the same again. He gained a compassionate heart, a taste for self-sufficiency and simplicity, and a knack for healing. The types of both Guzmán and Núñez are still among us. Another person has also walked onto the Noh stage of Turtle Island history to hold hands with Alvar Núñez at the far end of the process—Ishi the Yahi, who walked into civilization with as much desperation as Núñez walked out of it. Núñez was the first European to encounter North America and its native myth-mind, and Ishi was the last Native American to fully know that mind—and he had to leave it behind. What lies between those two brackets is not dead and gone. It is perennially within us, dormant as a hard-shelled seed, awaiting the fire or flood that awakes it again.

In those intervening centuries, tens of millions of North and South American Indians died early and violent deaths (as did countless Europeans), the world's largest mammal herd was extinguished (the bison), and fifteen million Pronghorn disappeared. The grasslands and their soils are largely gone, and only remnants survive from the original old-growth eastern hardwood and western conifer forests. We all know more items for this list.

It is often said that the frontier gave a special turn to American history. A frontier is a burning edge, a frazzle, a strange market zone between two utterly different worlds. It is a strip where there are pelts and tongues and tits for the taking. There is an almost visible line that a person of the invading culture could walk across: out of history and into a perpetual present, a way of life attuned to the slower and steadier processes of nature. The possibility of passage into that myth-time world had been all but forgotten in Europe. Its rediscovery—the unsettling vision of a natural self—has haunted the Euro-American peoples as they continually cleared and roaded the many wild corners of the North American continent.

Wilderness is now—for much of North America—places that are formally set aside on public lands—Forest Service or Bureau of Land Management holdings or state and federal parks. Some tiny but critical tracts are held by private nonprofit groups like The Nature Conservancy or the Trust for Public Land. These are the shrines saved from all the land that was once known and lived on by the original people, the little bits left as they were, the last little places where intrinsic nature totally wails, blooms, nests, glints away. They make up only 2 percent of the land of the United States.

But wildness is not limited to the 2 percent formal wilderness areas. Shifting scales, it is everywhere: ineradicable populations of fungi, moss, mold, yeasts, and such that surround and inhabit us. Deer mice on the back porch, deer bounding across the freeway, pigeons in the park, spiders in the corners. There were crickets in the paint locker of the *Sappa Creek* oil tanker, as I worked as a wiper in the engine room out in mid-Pacific, cleaning brushes. Exquisite complex beings in their energy webs inhabiting the fertile corners of the urban world in accord with the rules of wild systems, the visible hardy stalks and stems of vacant lots and railroads, the persistent raccoon squads, bacteria in the loam and in our yogurt. The term *culture*, in its meaning of "a deliberately maintained aesthetic and intellectual life" and in its other meaning of "the totality of socially transmitted behavior patterns," is never far from a biological root meaning as in "yogurt culture"—a nourishing habitat. Civilization is permeable, and could be as inhabited as the wild is.

Wilderness may temporarily dwindle, but wildness won't go away. A ghost wilderness hovers around the entire planet: the millions of tiny seeds of the original vegetation are hiding in the mud on the foot of an arctic tern, in the dry desert sands, or in the wind. These seeds are each uniquely adapted to a specific soil or circumstance, each with its own little form and fluff, ready to float, freeze, or be swallowed, always preserving the germ. Wilderness will inevitably return, but it will not be as fine a world as the one that was glistening in the early morning of the Holocene. Much life will be lost in the wake of human agency on earth, that of the twentieth and twenty-first centuries. Much is already lost—the soils and waters unravel:

> "What's that dark thing in the water?
> Is it not an oil-soaked otter?"

Where do we start to resolve the dichotomy of the civilized and the wild?

Do you really believe you are an animal? We are now taught this in school. It is a wonderful piece of information: I have been enjoying it all my life and I come back to it over and over again, as something to investigate and test. I grew up on a small farm with cows and chickens, and with a second-growth forest right at the back fence, so I had the good fortune of seeing the human and animal as in the same realm. But many people who have been hearing this since childhood have not absorbed the implications of it, perhaps feel remote from the nonhuman world, are not *sure* they are animals. They would like to feel they might be something better than animals. That's understandable: other animals might feel they are something different than "just animals" too. But we must contemplate the shared ground of our common biological being before emphasizing the differences.

Our bodies are wild. The involuntary quick turn of the head at a shout, the vertigo at looking off a precipice, the heart-in-the-throat in a moment of danger, the catch of the breath, the quiet moments relaxing, staring, reflecting—all universal responses of this mammal body. They can be seen throughout the class. The body does not require the intercession of some conscious intellect to make it breathe, to keep the heart beating. It is to a great extent self-regulating, it is a life of its own. Sensation and perception do not exactly come from outside, and the unremitting thought and image-flow are not exactly outside. The world is our consciousness, and it surrounds us. There are more things in mind, in the imagination, than "you" can keep track of—thoughts, memories, images, angers, delights, rise unbidden. The depths of mind, the unconscious, are our inner wilderness areas, and that is where a bobcat is *right now*. I do not mean personal bobcats in personal psyches, but the bobcat that roams from dream to dream. The conscious agenda-planning ego occupies a very tiny territory, a little cubicle somewhere near the gate, keeping track of some of what goes in and out (and sometimes making expansionistic plots), and the rest takes care of itself. The body is, so to speak, in the mind. They are both wild.

Some will say, so far so good. "We are mammal primates. But we have language, and the animals don't." By some definitions perhaps they don't. But they do communicate extensively, and by call systems we are just beginning to grasp.

It would be a mistake to think that human beings got "smarter" at some point and invented first language and then society. Language and culture emerge from our biological-social natural existence, animals that we were/are. Language is a mind-body system that coevolved with our needs and nerves. Like imagination and the body, language rises unbidden. It is of a complexity that eludes our rational intellectual capacities. All attempts at scientific description of natural languages have fallen short of completeness, as the descriptive linguists readily confess, yet the child learns the mother tongue early and has virtually mastered it by six.

Language is learned in the house and in the fields, not at school. Without having ever been taught formal grammar we utter syntactically correct sentences, one after another, for all the waking hours of the years of our life. Without conscious device we constantly reach into the vast word-hoards in the depths of the wild unconscious. We cannot as individuals or even as a species take credit for this power. It came from someplace else: from the way clouds divide and mingle (and the arms of energy that coil first back and then forward), from the way the many flowerlets of a composite blossom divide and redivide, from the gleaming calligraphy of the ancient riverbeds under present riverbeds of the Yukon River streaming out the Yukon flats, from the wind in the pine needles, from the chuckles of grouse in the ceanothus bushes.

Language teaching in schools is a matter of corralling off a little of the language-behavior territory and cultivating a few favorite features—culturally defined elite forms that will help you apply for a job or give you social credibility at a party. One might even learn how to produce the byzantine artifact known as the professional paper. There are many excellent reasons to master these things, but the power, the *virtu*, remains on the side of the wild.

Social order is found throughout nature—long before the age of books and legal codes. It is inherently part of what we are, and its patterns follow the same foldings, checks and balances, as flesh or stone. What we call social organization and order in government is a set of forms that have been appropriated by the calculating mind from the operating principles in nature.

The World Is Watching

The world is as sharp as the edge of a knife—a Northwest Coast saying. Now how does it look from the standpoint of peoples for whom there is no great dichotomy between their culture and nature, those who live in societies whose economies draw on uncultivated systems? The pathless world of wild nature is a surpassing school and those who have lived through her can be tough and funny teachers. Out here one is in constant engagement with countless plants and animals. To be well educated is to have learned the songs, proverbs, stories, sayings, myths (and technologies) that come with this experiencing of the nonhuman members of the local ecological community. Practice in the field, "open country," is foremost. Walking is the great adventure, the first meditation, a practice of heartiness and soul primary to humankind. Walking is the exact balance of spirit and humility. Out walking, one notices where there is food. And there are firsthand true stories of "Your ass is somebody else's meal"—a blunt way of saying interdependence, interconnection, "ecology," on the level where it counts, also a teaching of mindfulness and preparedness. There is an extraordinary teaching of specific plants and animals and their uses, empirical and impeccable, that never reduces them to objects and commodities.

It seems that a short way back in the history of occidental ideas there was a fork in the trail. The line of thought that is signified by the names of Descartes, Newton, and Hobbes (saying that life in a primary society is "nasty, brutish, and short"—all of them city-

dwellers) was a profound rejection of the organic world. For a reproductive universe they substituted a model of sterile mechanism and
an economy of "production." These thinkers were as hysterical
about "chaos" as their predecessors, the witch-hunt prosecutors of
only a century before, were about "witches." They not only didn't
enjoy the possibility that the world is as sharp as the edge of a knife,
they wanted to take that edge away from nature. Instead of making
the world safer for humankind, the foolish tinkering with the powers of life and death by the occidental scientist-engineer-ruler puts
the whole planet on the brink of degradation. Most of humanity—
foragers, peasants, or artisans—has always taken the other fork.
That is to say, they have understood the play of the real world, with
all its suffering, not in simple terms of "nature red in tooth and claw"
but through the celebration of the gift-exchange quality of our give-
and-take. "What a big potlatch we are all members of!" To acknowledge that each of us at the table will eventually be part of the meal is
not just being "realistic." It is allowing the sacred to enter and accepting the sacramental aspect of our shaky temporary personal
being.

The world is watching: one cannot walk through a meadow or forest without a ripple of report spreading out from one's passage. The
thrush darts back, the jay squalls, a beetle scuttles under the grasses,
and the signal is passed along. Every creature knows when a hawk is
cruising or a human strolling. The information passed through the
system is intelligence.

In Hindu and Buddhist iconography an animal trace is registered
on the images of the Deities or Buddhas and Bodhisattvas. Manjusri
the Bodhisattva of Discriminating Wisdom rides a lion, Samantab-
hadra the Bodhisattva of Kindness rides an elephant, Sarasvati the
Goddess of Music and Learning rides a peacock, Shiva relaxes in the
company of a snake and a bull. Some wear tiny animals in their
crowns or hair. In this ecumenical spiritual ecology it is suggested
that the other animals occupy spiritual as well as "thermodynamic"

niches. Whether or not their consciousness is identical with that of the humans is a moot point. Why should the peculiarities of human consciousness be the narrow standard by which other creatures are judged? "Whoever told people that 'Mind' means thoughts, opinions, ideas, and concepts? Mind means trees, fence posts, tiles, and grasses," says Dōgen (the philosopher and founder of the Sōtō school of Japanese Zen) in his funny cryptic way.

We are all capable of extraordinary transformations. In myth and story these changes are animal-to-human, human-to-animal, animal-to-animal, or even farther leaps. The essential nature remains clear and steady through these changes. So the animal icons of the Inupiaq people ("Eskimos") of the Bering Sea (here's the reverse!) have a tiny human face sewn into the fur, or under the feathers, or carved on the back or breast or even inside the eye, peeping out. This is the *inua*, which is often called "spirit" but could just as well be termed the "essential nature" of that creature. It remains the same face regardless of the playful temporary changes. Just as Buddhism has chosen to represent our condition by presenting an image of a steady, solid, gentle, meditating human figure seated in the midst of the world of phenomena, the Inupiaq would present a panoply of different creatures, each with a little hidden human face. This is not the same as anthropocentrism or human arrogance. It is a way of saying that each creature is a spirit with an intelligence as brilliant as our own. The Buddhist iconographers hide a little animal face in the hair of the human to remind us that we see with archetypal wilderness eyes as well.

The world is not only watching, it is listening too. A rude and thoughtless comment about a Ground Squirrel or a Flicker or a Porcupine will not go unnoticed. Other beings (the instructors from the old ways tell us) do not mind being killed and eaten as food, but they expect us to say please, and thank you, and they hate to see themselves wasted. The precept against needlessly taking life is inevitably the first and most difficult of commandments. In their practice of killing and eating with gentleness and thanks, the primary peoples are our teachers: the attitude toward animals, and their treatment, in twentieth-century American industrial meat production is literally sickening, unethical, and a source of boundless bad luck for this society.

An ethical life is one that is mindful, mannerly, and has style. Of all moral failings and flaws of character, the worst is stinginess of thought, which includes meanness in all its forms. Rudeness in thought or deed toward others, toward nature, reduces the chances of conviviality and interspecies communication, which are essential to physical and spiritual survival. Richard Nelson, a student of Indian ways, has said that an Athapaskan mother might tell her little girl, "Don't point at the mountain! It's rude!" One must not waste, or be careless, with the bodies or the parts of any creature one has hunted or gathered. One must not boast, or show much pride in accomplishment, and one must not take one's skill for granted. Wastefulness and carelessness are caused by stinginess of spirit, an ungracious unwillingness to complete the gift-exchange transaction. (These rules are also particularly true for healers, artists, and gamblers.)

Perhaps one should not talk (or write) too much about the wild world: it may be that it embarrasses other animals to have attention called to them. A sensibility of this sort might help explain why there is so little "landscape poetry" from the cultures of the old ways. Nature description is a kind of writing that comes with civilization and its habits of collection and classification. Chinese landscape poetry begins around the fifth century A.D. with the work of Hsieh Ling-yun. There were fifteen hundred years of Chinese song and poetry before him (allowing as the *Shi-jing*—China's first collection of poems and songs, "The Book of Songs"—might register some five centuries of folksong prior to the writing down) and there is much nature, but no broad landscapes: it is about mulberry trees, wild edible greens, threshing, the forager and farmer's world up close. By Hsieh's time the Chinese had become removed enough from their own mountains and rivers to aestheticize them. This doesn't mean that people of the old ways don't appreciate the view, but they have a different point of view.

The same kind of cautions apply to the stories or songs one might tell about oneself. Malcolm Margolin, publisher of *News from Native California*, points out that the original people of California did not easily recount an "autobiography." The details of their individual lives, they said, were unexceptional: the only events that bore recounting were descriptions of a few of their outstanding dreams and their moments of encounter with the spirit world and its transformations. The telling of their life stories, then, was very brief. They told of dream, insight, and healing.

Back Home

The etiquette of the wild world requires not only generosity but a good-humored toughness that cheerfully tolerates discomfort, an appreciation of everyone's fragility, and a certain modesty. Good quick blueberry picking, the knack of tracking, getting to where the fishing's good ("an angry man cannot catch a fish"), reading the surface of the sea or sky—these are achievements not to be gained by mere effort. Mountaineering has the same quality. These moves take practice, which calls for a certain amount of self-abnegation, and intuition, which takes emptying of yourself. Great insights have come to some people only after they reached the point where they had nothing left. Alvar Núñez Cabeza de Vaca became unaccountably deepened after losing his way and spending several winter nights sleeping naked in a pit in the Texas desert under a north wind. He truly had reached the point where he had nothing. ("To have nothing, you must *have nothing*!" Lord Buckley says of this moment.) After that he found himself able to heal sick native people he met on his way westward. His fame spread ahead of him. Once he had made his way back to Mexico and was again a civilized Spaniard he found he had lost his power of healing—not just the ability to heal, but the *will* to heal, which is the will to be whole: for as he said, there were "real doctors" in the city, and he began to doubt his powers. To resolve the dichotomy of the civilized and the wild, we must first resolve to be whole.

One may reach such a place as Alvar Núñez by literally losing everything. Painful and dangerous experiences often transform the people who survive them. Human beings are audacious. They set out to have adventures and try to do more than perhaps they should. So by practicing yogic austerities or monastic disciplines, some people make a structured attempt at having nothing. Some of us have learned much from traveling day after day on foot over snow-fields, rockslides, passes, torrents, and valley floor forests, by "putting ourselves out there." Another—and most sophisticated—way is that of Vimalakirti, the legendary Buddhist layman, who taught that by directly intuiting our condition in the actually existing world we realize that we have had nothing from the beginning. A Tibetan saying has it: "The experience of emptiness engenders compassion."

For those who would seek directly, by entering the primary temple, the wilderness can be a ferocious teacher, rapidly stripping down the inexperienced or the careless. It is easy to make the mistakes that will bring one to an extremity. Practically speaking, a life that is vowed to simplicity, appropriate boldness, good humor, gratitude, unstinting work and play, and lots of walking brings us close to the actually existing world and its wholeness.

People of wilderness cultures rarely seek out adventures. If they deliberately risk themselves, it is for spiritual rather than economic reasons. Ultimately all such journeys are done for the sake of the whole, not as some private quest. The quiet dignity that characterizes so many so-called primitives is a reflection of that. Florence Edenshaw, a contemporary Haida elder who has lived a long life of work and family, was asked by the young woman anthropologist who interviewed her and was impressed by her coherence, presence, and dignity, "What can I do for self-respect?" Mrs. Edenshaw said, "Dress up and stay home." The "home," of course, is as large as you make it.

The lessons we learn from the wild become the etiquette of freedom. We can enjoy our humanity with its flashy brains and sexual buzz, its social cravings and stubborn tantrums, and take ourselves as no more and no less than another being in the Big Watershed. We can accept each other all as barefoot equals sleeping on the same ground. We can give up hoping to be eternal and quit fighting dirt. We can chase off mosquitoes and fence out varmints without hating them. No expectations, alert and sufficient, grateful and careful, generous and direct. A calm and clarity attend us in the moment we are wiping the grease off our hands between tasks and glancing up at the passing clouds. Another joy is finally sitting down to have coffee with a friend. The wild requires that we learn the terrain, nod to all the plants and animals and birds, ford the streams and cross the ridges, and tell a good story when we get back home.

And when the children are safe in bed, at one of the great holidays like the Fourth of July, New Year's, or Halloween, we can bring out some spirits and turn on the music, and the men and the women who are still among the living can get loose and really wild. So that's the final meaning of "wild"—the esoteric meaning, the deepest and most scary. Those who are ready for it will come to it. Please do not repeat this to the uninitiated.

The Place, the Region, and the Commons

"When you find your place where you are, practice occurs."   DŌGEN

The World Is Places

We experience slums, prairies, and wetlands all equally as "places." Like a mirror, a place can hold anything, on any scale. I want to talk about place as an experience and propose a model of what it meant to "live in place" for most of human time, presenting it initially in terms of the steps that a child takes growing into a natural community. (We have the terms *enculturation* and *acculturation*, but nothing to describe the process of becoming placed or re-placed.) In doing so we might get one more angle on what a "civilization of wildness" might require.

For most Americans, to reflect on "home place" would be an unfamiliar exercise. Few today can announce themselves as someone *from* somewhere. Almost nobody spends a lifetime in the same valley, working alongside the people they knew as children. Native people everywhere (the very term means "someone born there") and Old World farmers and city people share this experience of living in place. Still—and this is very important to remember—being inhabitory, being place-based, has never meant that one didn't travel from time to time, going on trading ventures or taking livestock to summer grazing. Such working wanderers have always known they had a home-base on earth, and could prove it at any campfire or party by singing their own songs.

The heart of a place is the home, and the heart of the home is the firepit, the hearth. All tentative explorations go outward from there, and it is back to the fireside that elders return. You grow up speaking a home language, a local vernacular. Your own household may have some specifics of phrase, of pronunciation, that are different from the *domus*, the *jia* or *ie* or *kum*, down the lane. You hear histories of the people who are your neighbors and tales involving rocks, streams, mountains, and trees that are all within your sight. The myths of world-creation tell you how *that mountain* was created and how *that peninsula* came to be there. As you grow bolder you explore your world outward from the firepit (which is the center of each universe) in little trips. The childhood landscape is learned on foot, and a map is inscribed in the mind—trails and pathways and groves— the mean dog, the cranky old man's house, the pasture with a bull in it—going out wider and farther. All of us carry within us a picture of the terrain that was learned roughly between the ages of six and nine. (It could as easily be an urban neighborhood as some rural scene.) You can almost totally recall the place you walked, played, biked, swam. Revisualizing that place with its smells and textures, walking through it again in your imagination, has a grounding and settling effect. As a contemporary thought we might also wonder how it is for those whose childhood landscape was being ripped up by bulldozers, or whose family moving about made it all a blur. I have a friend who still gets emotional when he recalls how the avocado orchards of his southern California youth landscape were transformed into hillside after hillside of suburbs.

Our place is part of what we are. Yet even a "place" has a kind of fluidity: it passes through space and time—"ceremonial time" in John Hanson Mitchell's phrase. A place will have been grasslands, then conifers, then beech and elm. It will have been half riverbed, it will have been scratched and plowed by ice. And then it will be cultivated, paved, sprayed, dammed, graded, built up. But each is only for a while, and that will be just another set of lines on the palimpsest. The whole earth is a great tablet holding the multiple overlaid new and ancient traces of the swirl of forces. Each place is its own place, forever (eventually) wild. A place on earth is a mosaic within larger mosaics—the land is all small places, all precise tiny realms replicating larger and smaller patterns. Children start out learning place by learning those little realms around the house, the settlement, and outward.

One's sense of the scale of a place expands as one learns the *region*. The young hear further stories and go for explorations which are also subsistence forays—firewood gathering, fishing, to fairs or to market. The outlines of the larger region become part of their awareness. (Thoreau says in "Walking" that an area twenty miles in diameter will be enough to occupy a lifetime of close exploration on foot— you will never exhaust its details.)

The total size of the region a group calls home depends on the land type. Every group is territorial, each moves within a given zone, even nomads stay within boundaries. A people living in a desert or grassland with great visible spaces that invite you to step forward and walk as far as you can see will range across tens of thousands of square miles. A deep old-growth forest may rarely be traveled at all. Foragers in gallery forests and grasslands will regularly move broadly, whereas people in a deep-soiled valley ideal for gardens might not go far beyond the top of the nearest ridge. The regional boundaries were roughly drawn by climate, which is what sets the plant-type zones—plus soil type and landforms. Desert wastes, mountain ridges, or big rivers set a broad edge to a region. We walk across or wade through the larger and smaller boundaries. Like children first learning our homeland we can stand at the edge of a big river, or on the crest of a major ridge, and observe that the other side is a different soil, a change of plants and animals, a new shape of barn roof, maybe less or more rain. The lines between natural regions are never simple or clear, but vary according to such criteria as biota, watersheds, landforms, elevation. (See Jim Dodge, 1981.) Still, we all know—at some point—that we are no longer in the Midwest, say, but in the West. Regions seen according to natural criteria are sometimes called bioregions.

(In pre-conquest America people covered great distances. It is said that the Mojave of the lower Colorado felt that everyone at least once in their lives should make foot journeys to the Hopi mesas to the east, the Gulf of California to the south, and to the Pacific.)

Every region has its wilderness. There is the fire in the kitchen, and there is the place less traveled. In most settled regions there used to be some combination of prime agricultural land, orchard and vine land, rough pasturage, woodlot, forest, and desert or mountain "waste." The de facto wilderness was the extreme backcountry part of all that. The parts less visited are "where the bears are." The wilderness is within walking distance—it may be three days or it may be ten. It is at the far high rough end, or the deep forest and swamp end, of the territory where most of you all live and work. People will go there for mountain herbs, for the trapline, or for solitude. They live between the poles of home and their own wild places.

Recollecting that we once lived in places is part of our contemporary self-rediscovery. It grounds what it means to be "human" (etymologically something like "earthling"). I have a friend who feels sometimes that the world is hostile to human life—he says it chills us and kills us. But how could we *be* were it not for this planet that provided our very shape? Two conditions—gravity and a livable temperature range between freezing and boiling—have given us fluids and flesh. The trees we climb and the ground we walk on have given us five fingers and toes. The "place" (from the root *plat*, broad, spreading, flat) gave us far-seeing eyes, the streams and breezes gave us versatile tongues and whorly ears. The land gave us a stride, and the lake a dive. The amazement gave us our kind of mind. We should be thankful for that, and take nature's stricter lessons with some grace.

Understanding the Commons

I stood with my climbing partner on the summit of Glacier Peak looking all ways round, ridge after ridge and peak after peak, as far as we could see. To the west across Puget Sound were the farther peaks of the Olympic Mountains. He said: "You mean there's a senator for all this?" As in the Great Basin, crossing desert after desert, range after range, it is easy to think there are vast spaces on earth yet unadministered, perhaps forgotten, or unknown (the endless sweep of spruce forest in Alaska and Canada)—but it is all mapped and placed in some domain. In North America there is a lot that is in public domain, which has its problems, but at least they are problems we are all enfranchised to work on. David Foreman, founder of the Earth First! movement, recently stated his radical provenance. Not out of Social Justice, Left Politics, or Feminism did I come—says David—but from the Public Lands Conservation movement—the solid stodgy movement that goes back to the thirties and before. Yet these land and wildlife issues were what politicized John Muir, John Wesley Powell, and Aldo Leopold—the abuses of public land.

American public lands are the twentieth-century incarnation of a much older institution known across Eurasia—in English called the "commons"—which was the ancient mode of both protecting and managing the wilds of the self-governing regions. It worked well enough until the age of market economies, colonialism, and imperialism. Let me give you a kind of model of how the commons worked.

Between the extremes of deep wilderness and the private plots of the farmstead lies a territory which is not suitable for crops. In earlier times it was used jointly by the members of a given tribe or village. This area, embracing both the wild and the semi-wild, is of critical importance. It is necessary for the health of the wilderness because it adds big habitat, overflow territory, and room for wildlife to fly and run. It is essential even to an agricultural village economy because its natural diversity provides the many necessities and amenities that the privately held plots cannot. It enriches the agrarian diet with game and fish. The shared land supplies firewood, poles and stone for building, clay for the kiln, herbs, dye plants, and much else, just as in a foraging economy. It is especially important as seasonal or full-time open range for cattle, horses, goats, pigs, and sheep.

In the abstract the sharing of a natural area might be thought of as a matter of access to "common pool resources" with no limits or controls on individual exploitation. The fact is that such sharing developed over millennia and always within territorial and social contexts. In the peasant societies of both Asia and Europe there were customary forms that gave direction to the joint use of land. They did not grant free access to outsiders, and there were controls over entry and use by member households. The commons has been defined as "the undivided land belonging to the members of a local community as a whole." This definition fails to make the point that the commons is both specific land *and* the traditional community institution that determines the carrying capacity for its various subunits and defines the rights and obligations of those who use it, with penalties for lapses. Because it is traditional and *local*, it is not identical with today's "public domain," which is land held and managed by a central government. Under a national state such management may be destructive (as it is becoming in Canada and the United States) or benign (I have no good examples)—but in no case is it locally managed. One of the ideas in the current debate on how to reform our public lands is that of returning them to regional control.

An example of traditional management: what would keep one household from bringing in more and more stock and tempting everyone toward overgrazing? In earlier England and in some contemporary Swiss villages (Netting, 1976), the commoner could only turn out to common range as many head of cattle as he could feed over the winter in his own corrals. This meant that no one was allowed to increase his herd from outside with a cattle drive just for summer grazing. (This was known in Norman legal language as the rule of *levancy and couchancy*: you could only run the stock that you actually had "standing and sleeping" within winter quarters.)

The commons is the contract a people make with their local natural system. The word has an instructive history: it is formed of *ko*, "together," with (Greek) *moin*, "held in common." But the Indo-European root *mei* means basically to "move, to go, to change." This had an archaic special meaning of "exchange of goods and services within a society as regulated by custom or law." I think it might well refer back to the principle of gift economies: "the gift must always move." The root comes into Latin as *munus*, "service performed for the community" and hence "municipality."

There is a well-documented history of the commons in relation to the village economies of Europe and England. In England from the time of the Norman Conquest the enfeoffed knights and overlords began to gain control over the many local commons. Legislation (the Statute of Merton, 1235) came to their support. From the fifteenth century on the landlord class, working with urban mercantile guilds and government offices, increasingly fenced off village-held land and turned it over to private interests. The enclosure movement was backed by the big wool corporations who found profit from sheep to be much greater than that from farming. The wool business, with its exports to the Continent, was an early agribusiness that had a destructive effect on the soils and dislodged peasants. The arguments for enclosure in England—efficiency, higher production—ignored social and ecological effects and served to cripple the sustainable agriculture of some districts. The enclosure movement was stepped up again in the eighteenth century: between 1709 and 1869 almost five million acres were transferred to private ownership, one acre in every seven. After 1869 there was a sudden reversal of sentiment called the "open space movement" which ultimately halted enclosures and managed to preserve, via a spectacular lawsuit against the lords of fourteen manors, the Epping Forest.

Karl Polanyi (1975) says that the enclosures of the eighteenth century created a population of rural homeless who were forced in their desperation to become the world's first industrial working class. The enclosures were tragic both for the human community and for natural ecosystems. The fact that England now has the least forest and wildlife of all the nations of Europe has much to do with the enclosures. The takeover of commons land on the European plain also began about five hundred years ago, but one-third of Europe is still not privatized. A survival of commons practices in Swedish law allows anyone to enter private farmland to pick berries or mushrooms, to cross on foot, and to camp out of sight of the house. Most of the former commons land is now under the administration of government land agencies.

A commons model can still be seen in Japan, where there are farm villages tucked in shoestring valleys, rice growing in the *tanbo* on the bottoms, and the vegetable plots and horticulture located on the slightly higher ground. The forested hills rising high above the valleys are the commons—in Japanese called *iriai*, "joint entry." The boundary between one village and the next is often the very crests of the ridges. On the slopes of Mt. Hiei in Kyoto prefecture, north of the remote Tendai Buddhist training temples of Yokkawa, I came on men and women of Ohara village bundling up slender brush-cuttings for firewood. They were within the village land. In the innermost mountains of Japan there are forests that are beyond the reach of the use of any village. In early feudal times they were still occupied by remnant hunting peoples, perhaps Japanese-Ainu mixed-blood survivors. Later some of these wildlands were appropriated by the government and declared "Imperial Forests." Bears became extinct in England by the thirteenth century, but they are still found throughout the more remote Japanese mountains, even occasionally just north of Kyoto.

In China the management of mountain lands was left largely to the village councils—all the central government wanted was taxes. Taxes were collected in kind, and local specialties were highly prized. The demands of the capital drew down Kingfisher feathers, Musk Deer glands, Rhinoceros hides, and other exotic products of the mountains and streams, as well as rice, timber, and silk. The village councils may have resisted overexploitation of their resources, but when the edge of spreading deforestation reached their zone (the fourteenth century seems to be a turning point for the forests of heartland China), village land management crumbled. Historically, the seizure of the commons—east or west—by either the central government or entrepreneurs from the central economy has resulted in degradation of wild lands and agricultural soils. There is sometimes good reason to kill the Golden Goose: the quick profits can be reinvested elsewhere at a higher return.

In the United States, as fast as the Euro-American invaders forcefully displaced the native inhabitants from their own sorts of traditional commons, the land was opened to the new settlers. In the arid West, however, much land was never even homesteaded, let alone patented. The native people who had known and loved the white deserts and blue mountains were now scattered or enclosed on reservations, and the new inhabitants (miners and a few ranchers) had neither the values nor the knowledge to take care of the land. An enormous area was de facto public domain, and the Forest Service, the Park Service, and the Bureau of Land Management were formed to manage it. (The same sorts of land in Canada and Australia are called "Crown Lands," a reflection of the history of English rulers trying to wrest the commons from the people.)

In the contemporary American West the people who talk about a "sagebrush rebellion" might sound as though they were working for a return of commons land to local control. The truth is the sagebrush rebels have a lot yet to learn about the place—they are still relative newcomers, and their motives are not stewardship but development. Some westerners are beginning to think in long-range terms, and these don't argue for privatization but for better range management and more wilderness preservation.

The environmental history of Europe and Asia seems to indicate that the best management of commons land was that which was locally based. The ancient severe and often irreversible deforestation of the Mediterranean Basin was an extreme case of the misuse of the commons by the forces that had taken its management away from regional villages (Thirgood, 1981). The situation in America in the nineteenth and early twentieth centuries was the reverse. The truly local people, the Native Americans, were decimated and demoralized, and the new population was composed of adventurers and entrepreneurs. Without some federal presence the poachers, cattle grazers, and timber barons would have had a field day. Since about 1960 the situation has turned again: the agencies that were once charged with conservation are increasingly perceived as accomplices of the extractive industries, and local people—who are beginning to be actually local—seek help from environmental organizations and join in defense of the public lands.

Destruction extends worldwide and "encloses" local commons, local peoples. The village and tribal people who live in the tropical forests are literally bulldozed out of their homes by international logging interests in league with national governments. A well-worn fiction used in dispossessing inhabitory people is the declaration that the commonly owned tribal forests are either (1) private property or (2) public domain. When the commons are closed and the villagers must buy energy, lumber, and medicine at the company store, they are pauperized. This is one effect of what Ivan Illich calls "the 500-year war against subsistence."

So what about the so-called tragedy of the commons? This theory, as now popularly understood, seems to state that when there are open access rights to a resource, say pasturage, everyone will seek to maximize his take, and overgrazing will inevitably ensue. What Garrett Hardin and his associates are talking about should be called "the dilemma of common-pool resources." This is the problem of overexploitation of "unowned" resources by individuals or corporations that are caught in the bind of "If I don't do it the other guy will" (Hardin and Baden, 1977). Oceanic fisheries, global water cycles, the air, soil fertility—all fall into this class. When Hardin et al. try to apply their model to the historic commons it doesn't work, because they fail to note that the commons was a social institution which, historically, was never without rules and did not allow unlimited access (Cox, 1985).

In Asia and parts of Europe, villages that in some cases date back to neolithic times still oversee the commons with some sort of council. Each commons is an entity with limits, and the effects of overuse will be clear to those who depend on it. There are three possible contemporary fates for common pool resources. One is privatization, one is administration by government authority, and the third is that—when possible—they become part of a true commons, of reasonable size, managed by local inhabitory people. The third choice may no longer be possible as stated here. Locally based community or tribal (as in Alaska) landholding corporations or cooperatives seem to be surviving here and there. But operating as it seems they must in the world marketplace, they are wrestling with how to balance tradition and sustainability against financial success. The Sealaska Corporation of the Tlingit people of southeast Alaska has been severely criticized (even from within) for some of the old-growth logging it let happen.

We need to make a world-scale "Natural Contract" with the oceans, the air, the birds in the sky. The challenge is to bring the whole victimized world of "common pool resources" into the Mind of the Commons. As it stands now, any resource on earth that is not nailed down will be seen as fair game to the timber buyers or petroleum geologists from Osaka, Rotterdam, or Boston. The pressures of growing populations and the powers of entrenched (but fragile, confused, and essentially leaderless) economic systems warp the likelihood of any of us seeing clearly. Our perception of how entrenched they are may also be something of a delusion.

Sometimes it seems unlikely that a society as a whole can make wise choices. Yet there is no choice but to call for the "recovery of the commons"—and this in a modern world which doesn't quite realize what it has lost. Take back, like the night, that which is shared by all of us, that which is our larger being. There will be no "tragedy of the commons" greater than this: if we do not recover the commons—regain personal, local, community, and peoples' direct involvement in sharing (in *being*) the web of the wild world—that world will keep slipping away. Eventually our complicated industrial capitalist/socialist mixes will bring down much of the living system that supports us. And, it is clear, the loss of a local commons heralds the end of self-sufficiency and signals the doom of the vernacular culture of the region. This is still happening in the far corners of the world.

The commons is a curious and elegant social institution within which human beings once lived free political lives while weaving through natural systems. The commons is a level of organization of human society that includes the nonhuman. The level above the local commons is the bioregion. Understanding the commons and its role within the larger regional culture is one more step toward integrating ecology with economy.

Bioregional Perspectives

The Region is the elsewhere of civilization.   MAX CAFARD

The little nations of the past lived within territories that conformed to some set of natural criteria. The culture areas of the major native groups of North America overlapped, as one would expect, almost exactly with broadly defined major bioregions (Kroeber, 1947). That older human experience of a fluid, indistinct, but genuine home region was gradually replaced—across Eurasia—by the arbitrary and often violently imposed boundaries of emerging national states. These imposed borders sometimes cut across biotic areas and ethnic zones alike. Inhabitants lost ecological knowledge and community solidarity. In the old ways, the flora and fauna and landforms are *part of the culture*. The world of culture and nature, which is actual, is almost a shadow world now, and the insubstantial world of political jurisdictions and rarefied economies is what passes for reality. We live in a backwards time. We can regain some small sense of that old membership by discovering the original lineaments of our land and steering—at least in the home territory and in the mind— by those rather than the borders of arbitrary nations, states, and counties.

Regions are "interpenetrating bodies in semi-simultaneous spaces" (Cafard, 1989). Biota, watersheds, landforms, and elevations are just a few of the facets that define a region. Culture areas, in the same way, have subsets such as dialects, religions, sorts of arrow-release, types of tools, myth motifs, musical scales, art styles. One sort of regional outline would be floristic. The coastal Douglas Fir, as the definitive tree of the Pacific Northwest, is an example. (I knew it intimately as a boy growing up on a farm between Lake Washington and Puget Sound. The local people, the Snohomish, called it *lukta tciyats*, "wide needles.") Its northern limit is around the Skeena River in British Columbia. It is found west of the crest through Washington, Oregon, and northern California. The southern coastal limit of Douglas Fir is about the same as that of salmon, which do not run south of the Big Sur River. Inland it grows down the west slope of the Sierra as far south as the north fork of the San Joaquin River. That outline describes the boundary of a larger natural region that runs across three states and one international border.

The presence of this tree signifies a rainfall and a temperature range and will indicate what your agriculture might be, how steep the pitch of your roof, what raincoats you'd need. You don't have to know such details to get by in the modern cities of Portland or Bellingham. But if you do know what is taught by plants and weather, you are in on the gossip and can truly feel more at home. The sum of a field's forces becomes what we call very loosely the "spirit of the place." To know the spirit of a place is to realize that you are a part of a part and that the whole is made of parts, each of which is whole. You start with the part you are whole in.

As quixotic as these ideas may seem, they have a reservoir of strength and possibility behind them. The spring of 1984, a month after equinox, Gary Holthaus and I drove down from Anchorage to Haines, Alaska. We went around the upper edge of the basin of the Copper River, skirted some tributaries of the Yukon, and went over Haines Summit. It was White and Black Spruce taiga all the way, still frozen up. Dropping down from the pass to saltwater at Chilkat inlet we were immediately in forests of large Sitka Spruce, Skunk Cabbage poking out in the swamps, it was spring. That's a bioregional border leap. I was honored the next day by an invitation to Raven House to have coffee with Austin Hammond and a circle of other Tlingit elders and to hear some long and deeply entwined discourses on the responsibilities of people to their places. As we looked out his front window to hanging glaciers on the peaks beyond the saltwater, Hammond spoke of empires and civilizations in metaphors of glaciers. He described how great alien forces—industrial civilization in this case—advance and retreat, and how settled people can wait it out.

Sometime in the mid-seventies at a conference of Native American leaders and activists in Bozeman, Montana, I heard a Crow elder say something similar: "You know, I think if people stay somewhere long enough—even white people—the spirits will begin to speak to them. It's the power of the spirits coming up from the land. The spirits and the old powers aren't lost, they just need people to be around long enough and the spirits will begin to influence them."

Bioregional awareness teaches us in *specific* ways. It is not enough just to "love nature" or to want to "be in harmony with Gaia." Our relation to the natural world takes place in a *place*, and it must be grounded in information and experience. For example: "real people" have an easy familiarity with the local plants. This is so unexceptional a kind of knowledge that everyone in Europe, Asia, and Africa used to take it for granted. Many contemporary Americans don't even *know* that they don't "know the plants," which is indeed a measure of alienation. Knowing a bit about the flora we could enjoy questions like: where do Alaska and Mexico meet? It would be somewhere on the north coast of California, where Canada Jay and Sitka Spruce lace together with manzanita and Blue Oak.

But instead of "northern California" let's call it Shasta Bioregion. The present state of California (the old Alta California territory) falls into at least three natural divisions, and the northern third looks, as the Douglas Fir example shows, well to the north. The boundaries of this northern third would roughly run from the Klamath/Rogue River divide south to San Francisco Bay and up the delta where the Sacramento and San Joaquin rivers join. The line would then go east to the Sierra Crest and, taking that as a distinct border, follow it north to Susanville. The watershed divide then angles broadly northeastward along the edge of the Modoc Plateau to the Warner Range and Goose Lake.

East of the divide is the Great Basin, north of Shasta is the Cascadia/Columbia region, and then farther north is what we call Ish River country, the drainages of Puget Sound and the Straits of Georgia. Why should we do this kind of visualization? Again I will say: it prepares us to begin to be at home in this landscape. There are tens of millions of people in North America who were physically born here but who are not actually living here intellectually, imaginatively, or morally. Native Americans to be sure have a prior claim to the term native. But as they love this land they will welcome the conversion of the millions of immigrant psyches into fellow "Native Americans." For the non-Native American to become at home on this continent, he or she must be *born again* in this hemisphere, on this continent, properly called Turtle Island.

That is to say, we must consciously fully accept and recognize that this is where we live and grasp the fact that our descendants will be here for millennia to come. Then we must honor this land's great antiquity—its wildness—learn it—defend it—and work to hand it on to the children (of all beings) of the future with its biodiversity and health intact. Europe or Africa or Asia will then be seen as the place our ancestors came from, places we might want to know about and to visit, but not "home." Home—deeply, spiritually—must be here. Calling this place "America" is to name it after a stranger. "Turtle Island" is the name given this continent by Native Americans based on creation mythology (Snyder, 1974). The United States, Canada, Mexico, are passing political entities; they have their legitimacies, to be sure, but they will lose their mandate if they continue to abuse the land. "The State is destroyed, but the mountains and rivers remain."

But this work is not just for the newcomers of the Western Hemisphere, Australia, Africa, or Siberia. A worldwide purification of mind is called for: the exercise of seeing the surface of the planet for what it is—by nature. With this kind of consciousness people turn up at hearings and in front of trucks and bulldozers to defend the land or trees. Showing solidarity with a region! What an odd idea at first. Bioregionalism is the entry of place into the dialectic of history. Also we might say that there are "classes" which have so far been overlooked—the animals, rivers, rocks, and grasses—now entering history.

These ideas provoke predictable and usually uninformed reactions. People fear the small society and the critique of the State. It is difficult to see, when one has been raised under it, that it is the State itself which is inherently greedy, destabilizing, entropic, disorderly, and illegitimate. They cite parochialism, regional strife, "unacceptable" expressions of cultural diversity, and so forth. Our philosophies, world religions, and histories are biased toward uniformity, universality, and centralization—in a word, the ideology of monotheism. Certainly under specific conditions neighboring groups have wrangled for centuries—interminable memories and hostilities cooking away like radioactive waste. It's still at work in the Middle East. The ongoing ethnic and political miseries of parts of Europe and the Middle East sometimes go back as far as the Roman Empire. This is not something that can be attributed to the combativeness of "human nature" per se. Before the expansion of early empires the occasional strife of tribes and natural nations was almost familial. With the rise of the State, the scale of the destructiveness and malevolence of warfare makes a huge leap.

In the times when people did not have much accumulated surplus, there was no big temptation to move in on other regions. I'll give an example from my own part of the world. (I describe my location as: on the western slope of the northern Sierra Nevada, in the Yuba River watershed, north of the south fork at the three-thousand-foot elevation, in a community of Black Oak, Incense Cedar, Madrone, Douglas Fir, and Ponderosa Pine.) The western slope of the Sierra Nevada has winter rain and snowfall and a different set of plants from the dry eastern slope. In pre-white times, the native people living across the range had little temptation to venture over, because their skills were specific to their own area, and they could go hungry in an unfamiliar biome. It takes a long education to know the edible plants, where to find them, and how to prepare them. So the Washo of the Sierra east side traded their pine nuts and obsidian for the acorns, yew bows, and abalone shells of the Miwok and Maidu to the west. The two sides met and camped together for weeks in the summer Sierra meadows, their joint commons. (Dedicated raiding cultures, "barbarians," evolve as a response to nearby civilizations and their riches. Genghis Khan, at an audience in his yurt near Lake Baikal, was reported to have said: "Heaven is exasperated with the decadence and luxury of China.")

There are numerous examples of relatively peaceful small-culture coexistence all over the world. There have always been multilingual persons peacefully trading and traveling across large areas. Differences were often eased by shared spiritual perspectives or ceremonial institutions and by the multitude of myths and tales that cross language barriers. What about the deep divisions caused by religion? It must be said that most religious exclusiveness is the odd specialty of the Judeo/Christian/Islamic faith, which is a recent and (overall) minority development in the world. Asian religion, and the whole world of folk religion, animism, and shamanism, appreciates or at least tolerates diversity. (It seems that the really serious cultural disputes are caused by different tastes in food. When I was chokersetting in eastern Oregon, one of my crew was a Wasco man whose wife was a Chehalis woman from the west side. He told me that when they got in fights she would call him a "goddamn grasshopper eater" and he'd shout back "fish eater"!)

Cultural pluralism and multilingualism are the planetary norm. We seek the balance between cosmopolitan pluralism and deep local consciousness. We are asking how the whole human race can regain self-determination in place after centuries of having been disenfranchised by hierarchy and/or centralized power. Do not confuse this exercise with "nationalism," which is exactly the opposite, the impostor, the puppet of the State, the grinning ghost of the lost community.

So this is one sort of start. The bioregional movement is not just a rural program: it is as much for the restoration of urban neighborhood life and the greening of the cities. All of us are fluently moving in multiple realms that include irrigation districts, solid-waste management jurisdictions, long-distance area code zones, and such. Planet Drum Foundation, based in the San Francisco Bay Area, works with many other local groups for the regeneration of the city as a living place, with projects like the identification and restoration of urban creeks (Berg and others, 1989). There are groups worldwide working with Third and Fourth World people revisualizing territories and playfully finding appropriate names for their newly realized old regions (*Raise the Stakes*, 1987). Four bioregional congresses have been held on Turtle Island.

As sure as impermanence, the nations of the world will eventually be more sensitively defined and the lineaments of the blue earth will begin to reshape the politics. The requirements of sustainable economies, ecologically sensitive agriculture, strong and vivid community life, wild habitat—and the second law of thermodynamics— all lead this way. I also realize that right now this is a kind of theater as much as it is ecological politics. Not just street theater, but visionary mountain, field, and stream theater. As Jim Dodge says: "The chances of bioregionalism succeeding . . . are beside the point. If one person, or a few, or a community of people, live more fulfilling lives from bioregional practice, then it's successful." May it all speed the further deconstruction of the superpowers. As "The Surre(gion)alist Manifesto" says:

> Regional politics do not take place in Washington, Moscow, and other "seats of power." Regional power does not "sit"; it flows every-

where. Through watersheds and bloodstreams. Through nervous systems and food chains. The regions are everywhere & nowhere. We are all illegals. We are natives and we are restless. We have no country; we live in the country. We are off the Inter-State. The Region is against the Regime—any Regime. Regions are anarchic. (Cafard, 1989)

Finding "Nisenan County"

This year Burt Hybart retired from driving dump truck, backhoe, grader, and Cat after many years. Roads, ponds, and pads are his sculpture, shapes that will be left on the land long after the houses have vanished. (How long for a pond to silt up?) Burt still witches wells, though. Last time I saw him he was complaining about his lungs: "Dust boiling up behind the Cat you couldn't see from here to there, those days. When I worked on the Coast. And the diesel fumes."

Some of us went for a walk in the Warner Range. It's in the far northeast corner of California, the real watershed boundary between the headwaters of the Pit River and the *nors* of the Great Basin. From the nine-thousand-foot scarp's high points you can see into Oregon, Goose Lake, and up the west side of the Warners to the north end of Surprise Valley. Dry desert hills to the east.

Desert mountain range. A touch of Rocky Montain flora here that leapfrogs over desert basins via the Steens Mountains of southeastern Oregon, the Blue Mountains, and maybe the Wallowas. Cattle are brought up from Eagleville on the east side, a town out of the 1880s. The proprietor of the Eagleville Bar told how the sheepherders move their flocks from Lovelock, Nevada, in early March, heading toward the Warners, the ewes lambing as they go. In late June they arrive at the foot of the range and move the sheep up to the eight-thousand-foot meadows on the west side. In September the flocks go down to Madeline—the lambs right onto the meat trucks. Then the ewes' long truck ride back to Lovelock for the winter. We find the flock in the miles-long meadow heavens of Mule-ear flowers. The sheep business is Basque-run on all levels. Old aspen grove along the trail with sheepherder inscriptions and designs in the bark, some dated from the 1890s.

Patterson Lake is the gem of the Warners, filling an old cirque below the cliffs of the highest peak. The many little ledges of the cliffs are home to hawks. Young raptors sit solemnly by their nests. Mt. Shasta dominates the western view, a hub to these vast miles of Lodgepole and Jeffrey Pine, lava rock, hayfield ribbons, rivers that sink underground. Ha! This is the highest end of what we call "upriver"—and close to where it drains both ways, one side of the plateau tipping toward the Klamath River, the other to the Pit and the Sacramento. Mt. Shasta visible for so far—from the Coast Range, from Sierra Buttes down by Downieville—it gleams across the headwaters of all of northern California.

Old John Hold walks up a streambed talking to it: "So that's what you've been up to!" Reading the geology, the wash and lay of the heavy metal that sinks below the sand, never tarnishing or rusting— gold. The new-style miners are here, too, St. Joseph Minerals, exploring the "diggings," the tertiary gravels. The county supervisors finally approved the EIR and the exploratory drilling begins. This isn't full-scale mining yet, and they'll come back in eighteen months with their big proposal (if they do). The drilling's not noticeable: a little tower and a trailer lost in the gravel canyons and ridges that were left from the days of hydraulicking.

There were early strong rains this fall, so the springs started up. Then the rain quit and the springs stopped. A warm December. Real rains started in January, with heavy snows above six thousand feet and not much below that. This year more kids go skiing. Resistance to it (as a decadent urban entertainment) crumbles family by family. Most adults here never were mountain people, didn't climb, ski, or backpack. They moved up from the city and like to think they're in a wilderness. A few are mountain types who moved down to be here, and are glad to be living where there are some neighbors. The kids go to Donner Pass to be sliding on the white crystals of future Yuba River waters. I get back to downhill skiing myself; it feels wonderful again. Downhill must have provided one of the fastest speeds human beings ever experienced before modern times. Cross-country ski trips in Sierra Buttes too. On the full moon night of April (the last night of the month) Bill Schell and I did a tour till 2 A.M. around Yuba Pass, snow shining bright in the moonlight, skis clattering on the icy slabs. Old mountain people turned settlers manage to finally start going back into the mountains after the house is built, the garden fenced, the drip-systems in. February brought ten inches of rain in six days. The ponds and springs stream over, the ground's all silvery with surface glitter of a skin of water. Fifteen feet of snow at Sugarbowl near Donner Pass.

Two old gents in the Sacramento Greyhound station. I'm next to an elder who swings his cane back and forth, lightly, the tip pivoting on the ground—and he looks about the room, back and forth, without much focus. He has egg on his chin. A smell of old urine comes from him, blows my way, time to time. Another elder walks past and out. He's very neat: a plastic-wrapped waterproof blanket-roll slung on his shoulder, a felt hat, a white chin beard like an Amish. Red bandanna tied round his neck, bib overalls. Under the overall bottoms peep out more trousers, maybe suit pants. So that's how he keeps warm, and keeps some clothes clean! Back in my traveling days men said, "Yeah, spend the winter in Sac."

I caught the bus on down to Oakland. In Berkeley, on the wall of the Lucas Books building, is a mural that shows a cross section of Alta California from the Northwest Coast to the Mojave Desert. I walked backward through the parking lot to get a look at it whole, sea lions, coyote, redtail hawk, creosote bush. Then noticed a man at one corner of it, touching it up. Talked to him, he is Lou Silva, who did the painting. He was redoing a mouse, and he said he comes back from time to time to put in more tiny fauna.

Spring is good to the apples, much fruit sets. Five male deer with antler velvet nubs walk about the meadow in the morning. High-country skiing barely ends and it's time to go fishing. Planting and building. This area is still growing, though not as rapidly as several years ago. The strong spirit of community of the early seventies has abated somewhat, but I like to think that when the going gets rough this population will stick together.

San Juan Ridge lies between the middle and south forks of the Yuba River in a political entity called Nevada County. New settlers have been coming in here since the late sixties. The Sierra counties are a mess: a string of them lap over the mountain crest, and the roads between the two sides are often closed in winter. A sensible redrawing of lines here would put eastern Sierra, eastern Nevada, and eastern Placer counties together in a new "Truckee River County" and the seat could be in Truckee. Western Placer and western Nevada counties south of the south fork of the Yuba would make a good new county. Western Sierra County plus a bit of Yuba County and northern Nevada County put together would fit into the watershed of the three forks of the Yuba. I would call it "Nisenan County" after the native people who lived here. Most of them were killed or driven away by the gold rush miners.

People live on the ridges because the valleys are rocky or brushy and have no level bottoms. In the Sierra Nevada a good human habitat is not a valley bottom, but a wide gentle *ridge* between canyons.

Tawny Grammar

The Same Old Song and Dance

I was standing outside the wood-frame community hall of the newly built St. Johns Woods housing project in Portland, Oregon, on a Saturday summer eve, 1943. It pulsed, glowed, and wailed like a huge jellyfish—there was a dance going on. Most of the people who had come to live in St. Johns Woods were working in the shipyards, but there were a few servicemen home on leave, and a lot of teenagers from the high school. Most of them were from the Midwest or the South. I was from farther north, up by Puget Sound, and had never heard people speak southern before. I hung around and finally got up my nerve to go in and listen to the live band play swing and jitterbug. At some point they were playing the Andrews Sisters song "Drinking Rum and Coca Cola." A girl from St. Johns high school saw me. I was a smallish thirteen-year-old freshman and she was a large gentle woman of a girl who (for what reason I'll never know) relentlessly drew me out on the floor and got me to dance with her.

I had no social confidence or experience. My usual pastimes were watching the migratory waterfowl in the sloughs along the Columbia River or sewing moccasins. The war and its new jobs had brought my family off the farm and into the city. I was first exhilarated and then terrified: as I reached around this half-known girl—taller than I—I could feel her full breasts against my ribs. My hand settled into the unfamiliar triangle at the base of her broad back and I smelled her sweet and physical odor. I was almost overpowered by the intuition of sexuality, womanliness, the differences of bodies. I had never danced before, never held a woman. I could barely get my breath. She simply kept me moving, swinging, swaying, with infinite patience, and as I got my breath back I knew I was, now, dancing. I exulted then, knowing I could do it. It was "our era, our dance, our song." I didn't dance with her again, she was soon gone with an older boy. But she had given me entry to the dance, and I had with astonishing luck passed a barrier of fear and trembling before the warmth of a grown woman. I had been in on adult society and its moment.

Each dance and its music belong to a time and place. It can be borrowed elsewhere, or later in time, but it will never be in its moment again. When these little cultural blooms are past, they become ethnic or nostalgic, but never quite fully present—manifesting the web of their original connections and meanings—again.

Maize, rice, reindeer, sweet potato—these indicate places and cultures. As plants they stand for the soil and rainfall, and as food sources they reflect society and its productive arrangements. Another indicator is the local "song and dance." The occasion of singers, musicians, storytellers, mask makers, and dancers joining together is the flower of daily life. Not only the human is danced, but raven, deer, cow, and rainstorm make their appearance. The dance enables us to present our many human and nonhuman selves to each other, and to the place. The place is offered to itself. Art and economics are both matters of gift-exchange and the dance-offering in particular has been a proper sort of trade for the taking of fruits, grain, or game. Such giving also helps us overcome our tendencies toward stinginess and arrogance.

Every traditional culture has its dance. The young people who come to the study of dance bring their peerless perennial grace and power. They must learn to count rhythm, memorize the chants, identify certain plants, observe the seasons, absorb the gestures of animals, and to move as timely as a falcon on a stoop. Thus they are borne by their culture to become culture-bearers. The yoga of dance (as the great Bharat Natyam performer and teacher Balasaraswati called it) can be one of the paths to self-realization.

But that's only the spiritual side of it. The middle or main part is the perpetual reincarnation of a sacramental sense of the world, and dance carries that forward. It's true that many people today do not quite have their own song and dance. Current music is too much a commodity, too much in flux, it cannot dye us. We are not quite sure what our home music is. When men drink together in Japan, at a certain point in the evening they begin to take turns singing the folksongs of their home provinces. When the American in the group is called on, he has a hard time knowing what to sing. (I used to sing the quintessential ballad of Puget Sound, "Acres of Clams.")

Because dance clearly has such cultural and religious significance it often comes under attack from the administrators for imperialist powers—or fundamentalist preachers or ayatollahs. When missionaries went into Inupiaq Eskimo territory—on the Alaskan coast of the Bering and Chukchi seas, and the northern coast of Alaska—in the last years of the nineteenth century, one of the first things they banned was dance. People there today still hunt, fish, sew mukluks, make birchbark containers, but there is no dance. A bit farther south on the Bering Sea coast is Yu'pik Eskimo territory. The Yu'pik-speaking people were missionized by the Russian Orthodox church, which did not ban dance. A dance revival has been going on in those villages—an invigorating cultural renaissance which is taking them away from TV sets and back to the community hall to rehearse and perform.

In Hawai'i the political renaissance of native culture has two strong cultural poles: a renewal of interest in the traditional techniques of taro-growing and ancient or *"kahiku"* hula. The hula teachers with their schools, called *halau*, accept students of all races but they insist that the students master Hawai'ian-language dance terminology. Students must memorize the oral epics in Hawai'ian, make their own costumes, and learn how to make offerings to Laka, Goddess of Dance. Its multicultural openness makes it possible for newcomers to have an entry into the traditional Hawai'ian sense of the islands.

Bharat Natyam, the dance of South India, is a confluence of archaic folk tradition, court patronage, northern-derived religious devotionalism, professional temple dance-offering, and twentieth-century cultural revival. The tradition has exceptionally high standards —the music alone is a lifetime study, the categories and qualities of gesture and expression are another study, and the accompanying drumming is a specialty of its own. The myth-derived narratives chanted to accompany certain dances evoke a vast and timeless cosmos. I didn't know all this when I first saw Padma Bhushan Shrimati Balasaraswati in a Bharat Natyam performance in Jaipur, India, in March of 1962. It was storming. We sat on the ground under a circus tent shaking in the wind, and then it began to rain in warm torrents and half the people left. The performance went on. I saw Bala act out, dance out, that moment when Krishna's mother—trying to remove the clod of dirt he's teething on from his baby mouth—looks in and sees not dirt but the depths of the whole universe and all its stars. She straightens up, backs away, in divine awe. To music. (This was Krishna's mischief on his mother.) My hair stood up.

I followed Bala to Bombay to watch her again, and was invited to a private late-night concert in an apartment. I asked Bala, "When you move in your dance to the point where you look into Krishna's mouth, are you already visualizing stars?" She laughed sardonically and said: "Of course not. I must start with dirt. It must become stars. Sometimes all I see is dirt, and the dance fails. That night it was stars."

Back on the west coast of North America ten years later we discovered that Balasaraswati—"Baby Saraswati" (Saraswati the goddess is the partner of Brahma and patron of poetry, music, and learning)—would be teaching classes in Berkeley. We connected with her, and I learned more about her tradition. Under English rule Bharat Natyam had been made virtually illegal because some of the dancers had served as Devadasis, "Servants of the God." These were young women who had been apprenticed to the Hindu temples in childhood to learn the dance. Their main role was in the presentation of daily dance-offerings in the inner shrine. An occasional part of the service to Shiva was to make love with very wealthy temple patrons. It is said that when they left temple service they made good marriages. The new laws totally forbade women to dance in Hindu temples.

Balasaraswati and her circle struggled to return Bharat Natyam to a position of respect within Indian society. The puritanized South Indian conservatives feared the erotic component, which Bala defended, purified, and resanctified. She was a yogini of dance. After a precocious start as a seventeen-year-old performer, she had a dark time for several years. It became her deep wish to dance before Shiva, known in the south as Murugan, in the temple of Tiruttani. She bribed the watchman, entered the inner chamber late at night, and danced alone in the shrine-room. She says she offered herself and her art to Shiva and to the world that night. Bala made a name for herself first in India and then in Europe and America. She traced the upturn in her fortunes to that dance within the shrine.

In Bala's repertoire was a folkdance that completed the loop from cosmic myth to village life. In South India the adolescents are charged with keeping parrots out of the ripening crops. The bird-chasing work is known as an occasion for trysting. The dancer sings and strolls forward and back through the gardens, waving a stick, startling up flocks of birds, to an old Telugu folksong chorus. The crops, the soil, the parrots, the work, the dance, and young love all come together. Much of the vernacular culture of South India is compressed into this one little performance.

The Kuuvangmiut and the Humanities

The Safeway store in Fairbanks, Alaska, stays open twenty-four hours a day, summer or winter. Virtually all the food in the stores of Alaska is flown in. We were shopping at 2 A.M., the second week of April, buying pineapples, mangoes, broccoli, and kiwi to take as gifts to friends in the Inupiaq villages of Shungnak and Kobuk. Next morning early Steve Grubis and I helped Tom George fuel his Cessna 182 and back it out and across the dirt road and onto the airstrip across from his place at China Marina. We flew north across the Yukon River and then west, along the southern edge of the Brooks Range and down the broad basin of the Kobuk River, which drains into the Chukchi Sea. It was all under snow. I had been reading about the archaeological site at "Onion Portage," so our scholarly pilot flew an extra twenty miles downstream to swing over a big oxbow in the river. As the plane turned on its side, looking straight down I got a glimpse of this 15,000-year-old campsite and homesite that possibly hosted people who had come walking the land bridge from Siberia. The Kobuk River valley has never been under glacier ice. There's a pre-Pleistocene sagebrush, *Artemisia borealis*, and a legume, *Oxytropus kobukensis*, that grow here and nowhere else in the world.

The plane turned back upriver and glided over a solitary moose. We landed on the snowy strip at Kobuk on wheels, not skis. I was there to meet some schoolteachers and native leaders to exchange thoughts on what the role of occidental myth, folklore, poetry, and philosophy might be for the rising generation in the villages. Steve Grubis and I had worked over these questions before. He is with the cross-cultural orientation program at the University of Alaska, and he had old connections along the Kobuk River too. Some twenty years earlier he had been running the river on a log raft which was destroyed in a rapids, and with great travail over several weeks he had made his way downstream to Kobuk village where he was generously fed, clothed, and rested. Steve was also friends with Hans and Bonnie Boenish, who taught the school in Kobuk and were going to put us up. It was a few hundred yards' walk to the village. A snowmobile pulling the mail sled accompanied us. The sun was bright on the red and yellow kids' clothes hanging on the clotheslines, frozen stiff. The tethered sled dogs set up a happy racket, and some children were just going back up the steps of the modular metal classroom from an outdoor play recess. The school thermometer said ten below zero. The modular classroom, up on piers, looked a world apart from the low log cabins each with its log meat-cache on stilts and a woodsmoke plume rising straight up from each chimney.

As remote as the upper Kobuk River is, accessible only by plane or dogsled in winter and barely accessible by boat coming upriver in the brief summer, there is a mine nearby. The area is called Bornite and it is supposed to contain some of the largest copper deposits in the world. Roads and railroads have been surveyed, and company research on logistics has been going on for many years. The Kobuk people, "Kuuvangmiut" in Inupiaq, are still very much involved in the subsistence economy. Many get government aid, but they all depend on fishing (dog salmon, whitefish, blackfish, grayling, shee) and the essential caribou hunt. In season there is duck soup. Some run traplines. Everyone picks quantities of blueberries in the fall—lots of tricks to picking, preparing, and keeping the blueberries, *asriaviich*.

Mining, when and if it comes, will bring great changes to their economic and social life and they know it. So Hans, Bonnie, Steve, and I were soon engaged in the perennial discussion of what a useful schooling would be. Hans and Bonnie have been there for several years and Hans has his own sleds and team. They have a deep respect and concern for their Kuuvangmiut neighbors and employers.

We were speaking as outsiders, of course. We could agree that it might be wise to schedule school so that the students could be released at crucial times in the cycle of the year and learn subsistence skills from their parents and elders. This might enable them to maintain a sustainable and relatively autonomous economy into the twenty-first century. The village people I talked to were divided: some wanted traditional skills to be maintained while others felt that it was too late and their children should be getting an education that would work for them as well in Los Angeles as in Alaska. "Traditional skills" does not simply mean staying with pre-contact technology, of course—modern tools and machines are very practical and are at work in the service of native peoples all over the north, helping them to live in place. An updated subsistence economy in the circumpolar arctic is quite feasible. But there is also a strong likelihood that tastes and appetites for commercial goods and the need for more cash would tempt the next generation to choose the role of wage-earners in a mining economy.

So these children should prepare to be mining engineers? The company will bring its own experts with it. Heavy equipment operator? Maybe. Computers? Computers are in all the schools of the Far North, along with video cameras. There may be more computer literacy in the schools of northwest Alaska than in those of Los Angeles. Even so, there is no guarantee that any school anywhere in the whole world can give a child an education which will be of practical use in twenty years. So much is changing so fast—except, perhaps, caribou migrations and the berry ripening.

The native people of northwest Alaska have been intent on clarifying their own value system in recent years. This effort is called the "Inupiaq spirit movement"—the revival of Inupiaq spirit. On the wall of the classroom of the Kobuk school was a poster-sized list of "Inupiaq values":

HUMOR

SHARING

HUMILITY

HARD WORK

SPIRITUALITY

COOPERATION

FAMILY ROLES

AVOID CONFLICT

HUNTER SUCCESS

DOMESTIC SKILLS

LOVE FOR CHILDREN

RESPECT FOR NATURE

RESPECT FOR OTHERS

RESPECT FOR ELDERS

RESPONSIBILITY FOR TRIBE

KNOWLEDGE OF LANGUAGE

KNOWLEDGE OF FAMILY TREE

These warm and workable values are full of "grandmother wisdom," the fundamental all-time values of our species. Given a little stretching here and there, they'd work anywhere. What's lacking maybe is a clear articulation of what values apply to difficult or different neighbors—the concern is for conditions within the Inupiaq family, not for how to get along with outsiders.

People today are caught between the remnants of the ongoing "grandmother wisdom" of the peoples of the world (within which I include several of the Ten Commandments and the first five of the Ten Great Buddhist Precepts) and the codes that serve centralization and hierarchy. Children grow up hearing contradictory teachings: one for getting what's yours, another for being decent. The classroom teacher, who must keep state and church separate, can only present the middle ground, the liberal humanistic philosophy that comes out of "the university." It's a kind of thinking that starts (for the Occident) with the Greek effort to probe the literal truth of myth by testing stories and theories against experience. The early philosophers were making people aware of the faculty of reason and the possibility of objectivity. The philosopher is required to conduct the discussion with both hands on the table, and cannot require that you ingest a drug, eat a special diet, or follow any out-of-the-way regimen (other than intelligent reflection) to follow the argument. I'd say this was a needed corrective in some cases. A kind of intellectual clarity could thus be accomplished without necessarily discarding myth. Keeping myth alive requires a lively appreciation of the depths of metaphor, of ceremony, and the need for stories. Allegorizing and rationalizing myth kills it. That's what happened later in Greek history.

Still, the fifth-century Greeks did not invent the critical attitude. Myth, drama, *and* community discussion and intellectual argument are virtually universal. What the Greeks did do was exteriorize their intellectual life, make it convivial and explicit, define consistency in thinking, and publicly enjoy it. They saw an active and articulate intellectual stance as both modish and practical, sharpening and refining their ability to fulfill the obligations of citizenship in a society where clear and convincing argument counted for much. The give and take of their friendships and schools laid the groundwork for a continuing attitude of study that became in time textual and archival. But a practical and analytical intelligence does not necessarily require formal dialectics. Early pottery and the kiln, early metallurgy, the elegantly designed kayak and umiak, the navigation of the Melanesians, are all the end products of accurate and practical thinking.

People who already have all the answers argue that the humanistic stance lacks moral decisiveness. There are always some who think that judgments must come down hard. In the thought of İndia, the world is said to be a matter of many viewpoints—*darshan* (view)— each of which appears convincingly complete and self-contained to the one who is within it. One Buddhist system resolved to have "no particular view" and to practice a sublimely detached objectivity. Even so this school of thought—Madhyamika—did not swerve from accepting the first precept, *ahimsa*, nonharming. (This precept is implied in the Inupiaq list under the headings of humility, cooperation, sharing, and respect for nature.) There is no place in the philosopher's enterprise where greed and hatred are given any kind of support or approval. It's also clear that the humanist is not necessarily an agnostic. Socrates' last act was to ask that his promised offering to the spirit realm be carried out: "I owe a cock to Asclepius." The philosopher might despise mystification, but will respect the mysteries.

By April the arctic days are already pretty long. It was still a kind of twilight at 11 P.M. when the conversation wound down, with the sun just under the northern horizon. The next morning Steve and I borrowed a sno-go and went off over snowdrifts and crust through the open White Spruce tundra and muskeg toward the mountains and the mines at Bornite. There's a low pass and just over that we came on the shut-up wooden tower and sheds of an old copper mine. Cables, rope, and chain drooped from spikes on the board walls, the Schwatka Range mountains hovered to the north in an ice crystal haze. We walked around the mine buildings in the snow, then returned back down the sno-go trail with a great view across the wide basin and its frozen clusters of trees. Sub-boreal taiga: White

Spruce, Black Spruce and treeless bogs, willow and birch. In two more weeks, one of the men had said, the ducks might be back.

When Steve Grubis stumbled half-dead into Kobuk twenty years before, he was taken in and befriended by the postmaster, Guy Moyers. We walked over to visit Guy, who would be in his eighties. He was still the postmaster and the post office was the front room of his little house. Linoleum floor, new iron wood-burning range, a desk of shelves, and scales for mail. A black-haired oriental-eyed infant in a springy toddler swing was hanging and jouncing by the stove. "My granddaughter," he said. A teenager entered behind us, just out of school, and he introduced Wanda, another granddaughter. Wanda went into a tiny room screened by a blanket and turned on a tape of the music that young people play from the tropics to Greenland. Guy's wife was working kneeling on the floor by the stove. She was fleshing a piece of hide with a scraper made from sharpened steel pipe. She smiled and introduced herself as Faith. One wall was lined with shelves of stitched, bent, folded, birchbark baskets, a craft of this region.

Guy only vaguely remembered Steve, but that did not slow our conversation as we drank coffee. Guy said he came here by accident: he was let off at the wrong lake by a plane fifty years ago. He found his way to Kobuk and has been here ever since. A photo on the wall of Guy and his wife when they were newly married: her fine strong-boned features, a beautiful smiling young Inupiaq woman, and Guy a handsome young man with all his hair. "I was born here seventy-two years ago," she said. "I've stayed here."

Suppose I was a teacher at Kobuk or Shungnak, I thought, and had to teach the culture and history of this civilization that is moving in on them. Maybe we would read Shakespeare, some Homer, one of Plato's dialogues. (They are already well versed in Protestant Christianity.) "This is what they valued century after century," I'd have to say. And then they would live to see a mining operation open up nearby. The day-by-day procedures and attitudes of businessmen and engineers reflect little of anybody's supposed Western Culture.

The experience of contradictions, like taking little doses of poison, would prepare them to survive in a tricky pluralistic society. Could they keep alive a glimmer of respect for the Greek accounts of long after-dinner debates between articulate friends? And also remember their own tales of god-animals forming relationships with human men and women? And should not the teachers uncover the greed and corruption of successive empires, veiled behind art and philosophy? Sitting through such conversations in log cabins in Alaska helped me understand what my own boys and the sons and daughters of my neighbors on San Juan Ridge in California are up against. It seems as though everything except mathematics and linguistics—and myth—will become obsolete.

American society (like any other) has its own set of unquestioned assumptions. It still maintains a largely uncritical faith in the notion of continually unfolding progress. It cleaves to the idea that there can be unblemished scientific objectivity. And most fundamentally it operates under the delusion that we are each a kind of "solitary knower"—that we exist as rootless intelligences without layers of localized contexts. Just a "self" and the "world." In this there is no real recognition that grandparents, place, grammar, pets, friends, lovers, children, tools, the poems and songs we remember, are what we *think with*. Such a solitary mind—if it could exist—would be a boring prisoner of abstractions. *With no surroundings there can be no path, and with no path one cannot become free.* No wonder the parents of the Eskimo children of the whole Kotzebue Basin posted the "Inupiaq Values" in their schools.

The poor literati, I was thinking. Have philosophers and writers and such always been ineffectual bystanders while the energetic power-players of church, state, and market run the show? In the shorter time scale, this is true. Measured in centuries and millennia, it can be seen that philosophy is always entwined with myth as both explicator and critic and that the fundamental myth to which a people subscribe moves at glacial speed but is almost implacable. Deep myths change on something like the order of linguistic drift:

the social forces of any given time can attempt to manipulate and shape language usages for a while, as the French Academy does for French, trying to stave off English loanwords. Eventually languages return to their own inexplicable directions.

The same is true of the larger outline of world philosophies. We (who stand aside) stand on the lateral moraine of the glacier eased along by Newton and Descartes. The revivified Goddess Gaia glacier is coming down another valley, from our distant pagan past, and another arm of ice is sliding in from another angle: the no-nonsense meditation view of Buddhism with its emphasis on compassion and insight in an empty universe. Someday they will probably all converge, and yet carry (like the magnificent Baltoro glacier in the Karakoram) streaks on each section that testify to their place of origin. Some historians would say that "thinkers" are behind the ideas and mythologies that people live by. I think it also goes back to maize, reindeer, squash, sweet potatoes, and rice. And their songs.

It is appropriate to feel loyalty to a given glacier; it is advisable to investigate the whole water cycle; and it is rare and marvelous to know that glaciers do not always flow and that mountains are constantly walking.

My own grandparents certainly didn't tell us stories around the campfire before we went to sleep. Their house had an oil furnace instead, and a small library. (My grandfather did once say to me: "Read Marx!") So the people of civilization read books. For some centuries the "library" and the "university" have been our repository of lore. In this huge old occidental culture our teaching elders are books. *Books are our grandparents!* This charming thought came to me while riding John Cooper's dogsled from Kobuk to Shungnak down the Kobuk River ice and up the banks and bluffs, cutting across the portages. My nose, toes, and fingers were numb. The creaking of the rawhide thongs that bind the sled and give it flex, the gamelan-like complex pattering of dog feet running out of step, and the swish of snow. The dogs panting, happy, bright-eyed, breath steaming, we were coasting on the energy of the wolf-dog joy to run in packs—to run and run.

The library looks a little more interesting in this light. Useful, demanding, and friendly elders are available to us—I think of Bartolomé de las Casas, Baruch Spinoza, Henry David Thoreau. I always liked libraries: they were warm and stayed open late.

Arriving at Shungnak, crossing the river ice, we were greeted by boys who shouted the names of each of John's dogs—he had raced in the Iditarod the previous year and was a local hero. Hans and Bonnie Boenish came up behind us with another sled and team. We took the dogs out of their traces and chained them each to their own little house, then boiled up frozen whitefish to a stew in a 55-gallon oil drum cookpot outside over a spruce fire. (I there recalled watching Hawai'ians boiling drums of taro to feed the pigs.) Serving a dollop of fish stew to each dog in his or her own metal bowl, I found myself chanting the Zen hall meal verses to myself. I was the server. It was like being back home at Ring of Bone Zendo at mealtime—

> Fish Stew is effective in ten ways
> To aid the dogs that pull sleds
> No limit to the good results
> Consummating eternal frolicking!

The sled dogs sung along to the *gatha* in an unstructured chorus of sweet mournful howls.

We walked over to our hosts—the teachers, Bob and Cora McGuire, in their little house below the bluff and on the beach of the frozen Kobuk River. It must have been about zero degrees, but the McGuire girls, Jennifer and Arlene, were playing in the thin sunshine.

Inside the house the oil-burning cook range was kept on low and the wood stove was always going. With long underwear, and wool halibut shirts over our sweaters, we all stayed warm enough. Red plastic containers full of water had been carried down the hill from the school. They were kept in the kitchen so they wouldn't freeze. Over coffee the stories went on—Bob has been teaching for many years. A while back he left the north for a year to study remote schools around the world. Cora is also a teacher and her people are Athapaskan. Bob and Cora met at the university.

"If we actually tried to teach the values of western civilization, we'd just be peddling the ideology of individualism, of human uniqueness, special human dignity, the boundless potential of Man, and the glory of success," I said, giving it another look. Isn't that finally the Oil Pipeline philosophy? ("Jewish Inwardness— Greek Narcissism—Christian Domination" is how Doug Peacock the Grizzly Bear scholar puts it.) After Protestantism, capitalism, and world conquest, maybe that's still what occidental culture comes to.

But it wasn't that way when Greek learning made its way back into history. From the standpoint of the lively Italian minds of the fifteenth and sixteenth centuries the message of the Greek texts was that human beings are freely intelligent, imaginative, physical, bold, and beautiful. "Pagan." "Poetic." Maybe not so great an infla-tion of the human race (except in the eyes of the church) but a redis-covery of secular culture and of human beings as natural beings in a natural world. At any rate, an excited and deep study of antiquity— as occidental thinkers have gone through several times over—is akin to an apprenticeship with traditional elders. The freshness of the Re-naissance slid into the stuffy Latin, Language, and Culture curricu-lum of the European middle classes. The fascination with personal-ity and possibility got lost in authoritarianism and smugness.

For the children's teachers—native or white—the opportunity to teach a little history, philosophy, or literature is welcome, whatever culture it comes from. The rural school teachers that I have met in the north willingly arrange for tribal elders to come to classes and strongly support the teaching of traditional culture. Some village leaders said they have come to sense that we are all in the same boat—occidental culture, with its punky advanced capitalism and conky socialism, as well as the ragtag remnants of the great paleolithic hunting and gathering dignities.

Maybe the humanists of Europe were not exactly on the side of the power elites. Superficially they served urban masters, but their "project," whether they clearly knew it or not, was at bottom a defense of the vernacular—because to think clearly we must avoid narrow interests or entrenched opinions, and village values are in implicit opposition to the special interests of corporations or capital or traders or centralized religious bureaucracies and other such institutions. Being regional, being in place, has its own sort of bias, but it cannot be too inflated because it is rooted in the inviolable processes of the natural world.

Philosophy is thus a place-based exercise. It comes from the body and the heart and is checked against shared experience. (Grandmother wisdom suspects the men who stay too long talking in the longhouse when they should be mending nets or something. They are up to trouble—inventing the State, most likely.) We make a full circle in acknowledging that it is necessary to pay attention to the village elders and also to the wise elders of the Occident who have been miraculously preserved through the somewhat fragile institution of the library.

I gave a poetry reading at the Kobuk school one night. That's when John Cooper first turned up. He had driven his dogs forty miles south from his cabin on the Ambler River to hear some poems. The word was out on the two-way radio. It set all the dogs in the world barking when his team glided in. I had met John at Colorado State in the early seventies when he was studying Range Management and becoming a wilderness defender. The audience was local native people and a few white teachers—many of whom had never heard poetry read aloud before. Later that evening we talked of the singer-drummers who accompanied the dancers and the similarity of their role to the work of poets. An Inupiaq couple who had also come in from outside the village for the reading commented on the antiquity of myth. Our ancestors, they said, told the same stories as the Greeks, and the people in India, and the rest of Native America. *We all had a classical culture.*

There were questions about the civilizations of the Far East, and I loaned a copy of Lao-zi's *Dao De Jing* to a thoughtful woman leader who was active in both native culture and the church. Two days later over coffee she returned it saying, "Old. That book's really wise and old. I didn't know the Chinese went back so far." I asked her about her involvement with the church, because I knew her also to be very strong on Inupiaq spirit revival. "It's nice to be part of something international too," she said. "I didn't know in those days about China or India and their thought. But because I'm in the church I have friends all over, and people I see when I go to Seattle."

Steve and I left Shungnak very early one morning. We rode on a couple of sno-gos to the strip, two ravens hopped around a dog sleeping on the snow, frosty air swept back to Old Man Mountain and even farther to the notch in the hills where the track goes to Bornite. There had been a basketball game at the school the previous night, and the girls of the village had come up to see the out-of-town team off. Two hung on the wings of the Ambler Airlines plane, crying and sobbing for their new boyfriends, as some slightly older girls scolded them for being uncool. Aboard the plane there was another team, headed for a game in Fairbanks, all girls—the "Ambler Grizzlyettes." As long as the price of oil stayed up in Alaska, the bush airlines could cover their nut on high school basketball.

"Prudhoe Bay," John Cooper said—"I used to work summers there. Guys at Prudhoe Bay working 'seven-twelve'—seven days a week, twelve hours a day. Blow it on cocaine."

Nature's Writing

One of the formal criteria of humanistic scholarship is that it be concerned with the scrutiny of texts. A text is information stored through time. The stratigraphy of rocks, layers of pollen in a swamp, the outward expanding circles in the trunk of a tree, can be seen as texts. The calligraphy of rivers winding back and forth over the land leaving layer upon layer of traces of previous riverbeds is text. The layers of history in language become a text of language itself. In Paul Friedrich's book *Proto-Indo-European Trees* he identifies the "semantic primitives" of the Indo-European tribe of languages through a group of words that have not changed much through twelve thousand years—and those are tree names: especially birch, willow, alder, elm, ash, apple, and beech (*bher, wyt, alysos, ulmo, os, abul, bhago*) (Friedrich, 1970). Seed syllables, *bija*, of the life of the west.

In very early China diviners heated tortoise shell over flame till it cracked and then read meanings from the design of the cracks. It's a Chinese idea that writing started from copying these cracks. Every kind of writing relates to natural materials. The current form of Chinese characters with their little hooks and right angles came about when the Han Chinese shifted from incising signs with a stylus on shaved bamboo staves to writing with a rabbit-hair brush dipped in a pine soot ink on absorbent mulberry-fiber paper. The Chinese character forms are entirely a function of the way a brush tip turns when it lifts off the page. Lifting a brush, a burin, a pen, or a stylus is like releasing a bite or lifting a claw.

Light planes like kites, wobbling in the winds. In the long days of the arctic spring, people fly any hour of the day or night. Cutting south of Bettles and then taxiing down and skidding in the snow. In Fairbanks, I went to visit Erik Granquist, a Finnish paleotaxidermist, to take a look at his finished reconstruction of the body of an earlier sort of bison that had died thirty-six thousand years ago. At that time it was still in the lab at the university. It was a smallish, beautifully tight, and filled-out animal whose hide now has a bluish cast. Erik's previous project had been a Wooly Mammoth in Poland that had been found where it fell into a salt deposit.

He showed me how to read the story of the Pleistocene bison: "It's on its four legs, crumpled straight down, because when a bison is killed it doesn't fall over on its side like a moose, it drops straight down. These scratches on the hide were done by the lion that attacked it from the rear. The lion was no different from a contemporary African Lion. You can see the claw marks, then the fang punctures. They are exactly the width of the teeth of the modern lion. There are also the marks on the nose and the claw marks under the jaw and on the neck that show a second lion held it by the nose and held the head down. Next, the way the hide was opened up shows that they ate it from the rear, taking the backstrap along the tail and spine, and then left it. They didn't eat the neck or head, so it stayed collapsed in place with just one line of hide torn open right along the backbone. Shortly after the lions were finished with it, the weather turned cold and it froze. It was fall. In the following spring (and it was on the north side of the slope), mud melting at the top of the slope avalanched over and covered the frozen bison, still on its four legs, and carried it into the permafrost and sealed it anaerobically where it stayed frozen until it was washed out by hydraulic mining a few years back."

Erik also told me how on his birthday and at the end of the reconstruction, he had sacramentally eaten a tiny bit of the flesh that had been frozen for millennia and then helicoptered to a freezer. This bison body, a lyric salvaged from a very ancient manuscript, can now be seen in a University of Alaska museum display, where it is called "Babe."

Western culture is very brief when measured against one time-transcending bison corpse, or the wandering calligraphy of a river down the Yukon flats, or the archaic circumpolar cosmopolitanism of the traditions that connect with the Kuuvangmiut people. Euro-American humanism has been a story of writers and scholars who were deeply moved and transformed by their immersion in earlier histories and literatures. Their writings have provided useful cultural—rather than theological or biological—perspectives on the human situation. The Periclean Greeks digested the Homeric lore, which went back to the Bronze Age and before. The Romans enlarged themselves by their study of Greece. Renaissance seekers nourished themselves on Greece and Rome. Today a new breed of posthumanists is investigating and experiencing the diverse little nations of the planet, coming to appreciate the "primitive," and finding prehistory to be an ever-expanding field of richness. We get a glimmering of the depth of our ultimately single human root. Wild nature is inextricably in the weave of self and culture. The "post" in the term *posthumanism* is on account of the word *human*. The dialogue to open next would be among all beings, toward a rhetoric of ecological relationships. This is not to put down the human: the "proper study of mankind" *is* what it means to be human. It's not enough to be shown in school that we are kin to all the rest: we have to feel it all the way through. Then we can also be uniquely "human" with no sense of special privilege. Water is the koan of water, as Dōgen says, and human beings are their own koan. The Grizzlies or Whales or Rhesus Monkeys, or *Rattus*, would infinitely prefer that humans (especially Euro-Americans) got to know *themselves* thoroughly before presuming to do Ursine or Cetacean research.

When humans know themselves, the rest of nature is right there. This is part of what the Buddhists call the Dharma.

Mother Leopards

The word *grammar* is used by language scholars to mean the description of the structure of a language and the system of rules that govern it. A grammar is like a basket that can hold sentences in that language which would all work. In earlier times language scholars confused writing with speech. This is evident in the word *grammar* itself—the Greek *gramma* means "letter" with the root *gerebh* or *grebh* "to scratch" (hence kerf, graph, carve). Grammar comes from *gramma techne*, "woven scratches." But it is quite clear that the primary existence of language ("tongue") is in the event, the utterance. Language is not a carving, it's a curl of breath, a breeze in the pines.

Metaphors of "nature as books" are not only inaccurate, they are pernicious. The world may be replete with signs, but it's not a fixed text with archives of variora. The overattachment to the bookish model travels along with the assumption that nothing of much interest happened before the beginning of written history. Writing systems do confer an advantage. Those with writing have taken themselves to be superior to people without it, and people with a Sacred Book have put themselves above those with vernacular religion, regardless of how rich the myth and ceremony.

From Fairbanks I went back south to Anchorage. One night Ron Scollon and I were in the Pioneer Bar in Anchorage: I was telling of our trip out the Kobuk River and he was bringing me up to date on what had been happening in the field of linguistics. Ron and Suzanne Scollon are professional linguists who have worked for years with the Athapaskan family of languages and have published papers based on the observation of language-learning by both Athapaskan and Caucasian infants in the subarctic villages. So I took up my idea with him—that language belongs to our biological nature and writing is just moose-tracks in the snow. "Ron," I said, "does language not in some sense belong to biology?"

Ron's response was basically the following lecture: "Wilhelm von Humboldt—probably with some influence from his brother Alexander—started the 'speciation' metaphor for both organic phenomena and language. Ever since, languages have been viewed as though each was a different species, and the earlier historical linguists used to talk about a kind of Darwinian competition among them. But in biology species never converge, they only diverge. All languages belong to the same species and can interbreed, hence they can converge. Interlanguage dynamics will not just be competitive, but also familial and ecological. There is no sort of evolutionary improvement to be inferred from language history either: all languages work equally well and each has its own elegances. There's no such thing as the 'fittest' among languages. English became an international language only by virtue of British and American adventurism. (English is a rich midden-heap of semi-composted vocabularies further confused by the defeat at the hands of the Normans—a genuine creolized tongue that lucked out in becoming the second language to the world.) The fact is that changes in language, vowel shifts, consonant shifts, tendencies toward simpler or more complex grammars, do not seem to be in response to any practical needs."

"Well—so evolutionary principles don't apply. What about ecological forces? Human beings are still a wild species (our breeding has never been controlled for the purpose of any specific yield), and would you agree that language is also wild? The basic structures are not domesticated or cultivated. They belong to the wild side of the mind." "Sure," he said. "But if language is just one species there must be some other creatures in your mind-wilderness it interacts with, because a wilderness is a system. If language is a Pleistocene bison, what's the lion?"

"Ha! If language is an herbivore," said I, "it's not at the top of the chain. One might say 'poetry' is the lion because poetry clearly eats and intensifies natural speech. But given that almost all of our thinking is colored by language, and poetry is a subset of language use, that can't be it. I'd say it was the unconditioned mind-in-the-moment that eats, transforms, goes beyond, language. Art, or creative play, sometimes does this by going directly to the freshness and uniqueness of the moment, and to direct unmediated experience."

Ron tested me with a Whorfian challenge: "Is there *any* experience whatsoever that is not mediated by language?" I banged my heavy beer mug sharply on the table and half a dozen people jumped and looked at us. We had to give up and laugh at this point, since it always seems to come back to an ordinary mystery. Our table was under the branching head of a caribou.

All of my acquaintances in the Alaskan intelligentsia, both native and white, have been involved in trying to keep the native languages alive. Michael Krauss, James Kari, Gary Holthaus, the Scollons, Katherine Peters, Richard and Nora Dauenhauer, Elsie Mather, Steve Grubis, teachers like the Boenishes, the ecologist-anthropologist Richard Nelson, have all taken the language-survival question to heart. Krauss, who is head of the Alaska Native Languages Center, is not optimistic—the youngest speakers of the native tongues grow older and older every year. The village of Kobuk is one of the strongest, but even there I was told the youngest speakers were in their late teens, and the kids on the schoolground played in English. Though there's a statewide program supporting bilingual education and there are excellent bilingual texts and teaching texts for all the native languages, they seem to be fading. Most of the native families seem to perceive English as the wave of the future and the source of potential economic success for their children, so they don't make an effort to speak Language at home. (In Australia I always heard whatever local tongue was under discussion referred to as "Language." "Does she speak Language?")

This may be a passing phase. The native languages might regain their strength. It would help if teachers and administrators who were educated in the United States, which is (outside of a few areas) massively monolingual, would understand that bilingualism is neither rare nor difficult. An administrator who dreaded high school Spanish when young cannot believe that a little Eskimo girl can easily be bilingual. In the past, the cosmopolitanism of the worldwide

mosaics of small bioregionally based nations was guaranteed by virtually universal multilingualism. An elderly Yu'pik man who died
on a caribou hunt several years ago—he drowned while crossing a
river—was reported to have been one of the last of the multilingual
older generation. He was known to speak Yu'pik, Dena'ina (an
Athapaskan language), Russian, English, and some Inupiaq.

To speak of an "ecology of language" might start with recognizing
the common coexistence of levels, codes, slangs, dialects, whole
languages, and languages even of different families—in one
speaker. John Gumperz (1964) describes the situation of a village in
North India where "local dialects serve as vernaculars for most villagers. There may also be some untouchable groups with distinct
vernaculars of their own. In addition to the vernaculars there will be
several argots. One form of the subregional dialect is used with traders from nearby bazaar towns. Other different forms may be employed with wandering performers or religious ascetics . . . wandering ascetics of the Krishna cult might use Braj Bhasa while
worshipers of Ram would use Avadhi. Standard Hindi is the norm
for intercourse with educated outsiders. . . . In business transac-
tions or when talking to educated Muslims, Urdu is called for. Fur-
thermore the educated people know English and there are others
who have at least some knowledge of Sanskrit" (p. 420).

So we are back in the villages. The local mix of dialects and standard languages is unique to the place. All are rooted in nature; but
their vines and creepers reach worldwide. (But tonight the people
out in the Alaskan bush, in McGrath, Kobuk, or Kiana, are watching TV off the satellite, maybe the same program that's playing
down at the end of the bar.)

That's where the classics might come in. The Classic provides a
kind of norm. Not the statistical norm of behaviorism but a norm
that is proved by staying power and informed consensus. Staying
power through history is related to the degree of intentionality, in-

tensity, mindfulness, playfulness, and incorporation of previous strategies and standards within the medium—plus creative reuse or reinterpretation of the received forms, plus intellectual coherence, time-transcending long-term human relevance, plus resonances with the deep images of the unconscious. To achieve this status a text or tale must be enacted across many nations and a few millennia and must have received multiple translations.

The immediate time frame of human experience is the climates and ecologies of the Holocene—the "present moment," the ten or eleven thousand years since the latest ice age. Within the traditional literatures there are probably a few complete tales that are *that* old, as well as a huge quantity of later literature composed of elements borrowed from the oldest tradition. For most of this time, human populations were relatively small and travel took place on foot, by horse, or by sail. Whether Greece, Germania, or Han China, there were always nearby areas of forest, and wild animals, migratory waterfowl, seas full of fish and whales, and these were part of the experience of every active person. Animals as characters in literature and as universal presences in the imagination and in the archetypes of religion are there because they were *there*. Ideas and images of wastelands, tempests, wildernesses, and mountains are born not of abstraction but of experience: cisalpine, hyperboreal, circumpolar, transpacific, or beyond the pale. This is the world people lived in up until the late nineteenth century. (When was worldwide population one-half of what it is today? The 1950s.)

The condition of life in the Far North still approaches the experience of the hunter-gatherer world, the kind of world that was not just the cradle but the young adulthood of humanity. The north still has a wild community, in most of its numbers, intact. There is a relatively small group of hardy individuals who live as hunters and foragers and who have learned to move with the mindful intensity that is basic to elder human experience. It is not the "frontier" but the last of the Pleistocene in all its glory of salmon, bear, caribou, deer, ducks and geese, whales and walruses, and moose. It will not, of course, last much longer. The Arctic Wildlife Refuge will be drilled for oil, and the Tongass Forest of southeastern Alaska has been roaded and logged beyond belief.

The New World north is a window into the European past: where do the sacred salmon of the Celts, the Bjorns and Brauns and Brun-(hilde) [*bhar*- bear]-s of northern European literature, the dolphins of the Mediterranean, the bear dances of Artemis, the lion-skin of Herakles come from but the wild systems that the humans lived near? The persistence of these marvelous creatures in literature and imagination tells us how important they are to the health of our souls.

Ron and I turned our conversation then to China. He and I share this double focus: we appreciate Alaska as the most open and wildest place in the north—and one of the wildest places left on earth—and China as the most thoroughly literary of civilizations. They are not so far from each other across the globe. Both look like they are each nearing the end of their own case. But China, destructive as its re-cent environmental history may be, is a great civilization that will perhaps stay vital by virtue of its tiny thread of surviving wildness (call it Miao songs and Chan poems), and something of Alaska may survive by converting its newly arrived Euro-American population into postindustrial wilderness lovers by the magic of its casual dan-ger, all-day darkness, all-night light, emptiness, uselessness, face-lessness, frozen breath, smoked fish. The Anchorage newspaper re-ported that two moose had been walking around in the shopping mall parking lots again—malls that are right up against the spruce forest that leads to the Chugach Mountains.

A young white woman asked me (this was another time): "If we have made such good use of animals, eating them, singing about them, drawing them, riding them, and dreaming about them, what do they get back from us?" An excellent question, directly on the point of etiquette and propriety, and putting it from the animals' side. The Ainu say that the deer, salmon, and bear like our music and are fascinated by our languages. So we sing to the fish or the game, speak words to them, say grace. Periodically we dance for them. A song for your supper: performance is currency in the deep world's gift economy. The other creatures probably do find us a bit frivolous: we keep changing our outfits, and we eat too many different things. Nonhuman nature, I cannot help feeling, is well inclined toward humanity and only wishes modern people were more reciprocal, not so bloody.

Gary Holthaus, a long-time Alaskan and director of the Alaska Humanities Forum, and I walked down to the basement of the Captain Cook Hotel for breakfast. I had attended their annual meeting the day before to make a report on my time among the Kuuvangmiut. (Back in the seventies when he and I traveled to the southeast Alaskan Yu'pik village of Aleknagik I saw him packing his copy of Marcus Aurelius.) We were still discussing some of the ideas from the previous day's meeting, and we weren't in a mood to be so kind to the humanistic project. We were saying that it had not really been all that concerned for the real life of myth, poetry, and value. The Greek thinkers *started* with an oral repository of amazingly lively songs and stories—the Homeric poems and Hesiod. But their humanistic studies turned into an oddly formalistic and cramped concern for language.

A niche had opened up in the spaces between shaman, priest, poet, and mythographer. That niche was the city, the small city-state. Thought in the city reflected a kind of contest: the poetic and mythic way of seeing that was common to the villages versus the daily argumentation and *reportage* that dominated town life. At bottom it was a contest between subsistence economies and surplus—the centralized merchants. So the philosophers—the Sophists—were instructors to the rich young men on how to argue effectively in public. They did a fine job. They are the Founding Teachers of the whole occidental intellectual lineage. Ninety percent of what all so-called humanists have done throughout history has been to fiddle with language: grammar and rhetoric and then philology. For two and a half thousand years they believed not only in the Word but in a correct format for it. And if some of the French are trying to take the Word apart right now, it's because they are in the same tradition with the same obsession. But there were some fine people in the tradition: Hypatia with her mathematical intellectual paganism and Petrarch, the first modern mountaineer and the first vernacular lyric poet, to mention only two.

There's nothing wrong with clear speaking and honest argumentation. "Nothing specially occidental or high class or educated about speaking well," Holthaus said. "I've been to hundreds of meetings, and a lot of them were in the bush. Yu'pik or Inupiaq or Gwi'chin people—they all talk freely and to the point. The women are powerful speakers too. They didn't learn that from reading Cicero in school."

Thoreau wrote of "this vast, savage, howling mother of ours, Nature, lying all around, with such beauty, and such affection for her children, as the leopard; and yet we are so early weaned from her breast to society." Is it possible that a society as a whole might stay on better terms with nature, and not simply by being foragers? Thoreau replies: "The Spaniards have a good term to express this wild and dusky knowledge, *Gramatica parda*, tawny grammar, a kind of mother-wit derived from that same leopard to which I have referred." The grammar not only of language, but of culture and civilization itself, is of the same order as this mossy little forest creek, this desert cobble.

In one of his talks Dōgen said: "To carry yourself forward and experience myriad things is delusion. But myriad things coming forth and experiencing *themselves* is awakening." Applying this to language theory, I think it suggests that when occidental logos-oriented philosophers uncritically advance language as a unique human gift which serves as the organizer of the chaotic universe—it is a delusion. The subtle and many-layered cosms of the universe have found their own way into symbolic structure and have given us thousands of tawny human-language grammars.

Good, Wild, Sacred

Weeding Out the Wild

My family and I have been living for twenty years now on land in the Sierra Nevada range of northern California. These ridges and slopes are somewhat "wild" and not particularly "good." The original people here, the Nisenan (or Southern Maidu) were almost entirely displaced or destroyed during the first few decades of the gold rush. It seems there is no one left to teach us which places in this landscape were once felt to be "sacred"—though with time and attention, I think we will be able to feel and find them again.

Wild land, good land, sacred land. At home working on our mountain farmstead, in town at political meetings, and farther afield studying the problems of indigenous peoples, I hear such terms emerging. By examining these three categories perhaps we can get some insights into the problems of rural habitation, subsistence living, wilderness preservation, and Third and Fourth World resistance to the appetites of industrial civilization.

Our idea of Good Land comes from agriculture. Here "good" (as in good soil) is narrowed to mean land productive of a small range of favored cultivars, and thus it favors the opposite of "wild": the cultivated. To raise a crop you fight the bugs, shoo the birds, and pull the weeds. The wild that keeps flying, creeping, burrowing in—is sheer frustration. Yet wild nature cannot be called unproductive, and no plant in the almost endless mosaics of micro and macro communities is ever out of place. For hunting and gathering peoples for whom that whole spread of richness, the wild natural system, is also their economy, a cultivated patch of land might seem bizarre and definitely not good, at least at first. Gathering people draw on the whole field, ranging widely daily. Agricultural people live by a map constructed of highly productive nodes (cleared fields) connected by lines (trails through the scary forest)—a beginning of "linear."

For preagricultural people the sites considered sacred and given special care were of course wild. In early agrarian civilizations, ritually cultivated land or special temple fields were sometimes considered sacred. The fertility religions of those times were not necessarily rejoicing in the fertility of all nature, but were focusing on their own harvest. The idea of cultivation was conceptually extended to describe a kind of training in social forms that guarantees membership in an elite class. By the metaphor of "spiritual cultivation" a holy man has weeded out the wild from his nature. This is agrarian theology. But weeding out the wild from the natures of members of the *Bos* and *Sus* clans—cattle and pigs—gradually changed animals which are intelligent and alert in the wild into sluggish meat-making machines.

Certain groves from the original forest lingered on into classical times as "shrines." They were viewed with much ambivalence by the rulers from the metropole. They survived because the people who worked the land still half-heard the call of the old ways, and lore that predated agriculture was still whispered around. The kings of Israel began to cut down the sacred groves, and the Christians finished the job. The idea that "wild" might also be "sacred" returned to the Occident only with the Romantic movement. This nineteenth-century rediscovery of wild nature is a complex European phenomenon—a reaction against formalistic rationalism and enlightened despotism that invoked feeling, instinct, new nationalisms, and a sentimentalized folk culture. It is only from very old place-centered cultures that we hear of sacred groves, sacred land, in a context of genuine belief and practice. Part of that context is the tradition of the commons: "good" land becomes private property; the wild and the sacred are shared.

Throughout the world the original inhabitants of desert, jungle, and forest are facing relentless waves of incursions into their remotest territories. These lands, whether by treaty or by default, were left in their use because the dominant society thought the arctic tundra or arid desert or jungle forest "no good." Native people everywhere are now conducting an underprivileged and underfunded fight against unimaginably wealthy corporations to resist logging or oil exploration or uranium mining on their own land. They persist in these struggles not just because it has always been their home, but also because some places in it are sacred to them. This last aspect makes them struggle desperately to resist the powerful temptation to sell out—to take the cash and accept relocation. And sometimes the temptations and confusion are too great, and they do surrender and leave.

Thus some very cogent and current political questions surround the traditional religious use of certain spots. I was at the University of Montana in the spring of 1982 on a program with Russell Means, the American Indian Movement founder and activist, who was trying to get support for the Yellow Thunder Camp of Lakota and other Indian people of the Black Hills. Thunder Camp was on traditional tribal land that was under Forest Service jurisdiction at the time. These people wanted to block further expansion of mining into the Black Hills. Their argument was that the particular place they were reoccupying is not only ancestral but sacred.

During his term in office California Governor Jerry Brown created the Native American Heritage Commission specifically for California Indians, and a number of elders were charged with the task of locating and protecting sacred sites and native graves in California. This was done partly to head off confrontations between native people versus landowners or public land managers who start developments on what is now considered their property. The trouble often involves traditional grave sites. It was a sensitive move, and though barely comprehensible to the white voters, it sent a ripple of appreciation through all the native communities. Although the white Christian founders of the United States were probably not considering American Indian beliefs when they guaranteed freedom of religion, some court decisions over the years have given support to certain Native American churches. The connection of religion to *land*, however, has been resisted by the dominant culture and the courts. This ancient aspect of religious worship remains virtually incomprehensible to Euro-Americans. Indeed it might: if even some small bits of land are considered sacred, then they are forever not for sale and *not for taxing*. This is a deep threat to the assumptions of an endlessly expansive materialist economy.

Waterholes

In the hunting and gathering way of life, the whole territory of a given group is fairly equally experienced by everyone. Those wild and sacred spots have many uses. There are places where women go for seclusion, places where the bodies of the dead are taken, and spots where young men and women are called for special instruction. Such places are numinous, loaded with meaning and power. The memories of such spots are very long. Nanao Sakaki, John Stokes, and I were in Australia in the fall of 1981 at the invitation of the Aboriginal Arts Board doing some teaching, poetry readings, and workshops with both aboriginal leaders and children. Much of the time we were in the central Australian desert south and west of Alice Springs, first into Pitjantjara tribal territory and then three hundred miles northwest into Pintubi lands. The aboriginal people in the central desert all still speak their languages. Their religion is fairly intact, and most young men are still initiated at fourteen, even the ones who go to high school at Alice Springs. They leave the high school for a year and are taken into the bush to learn bush ways on foot, to master the lore of landscapes and plants and animals, and finally to undergo initiation.

We were traveling by truck over dirt track west from Alice Springs in the company of a Pintubi elder named Jimmy Tjungurrayi. As we rolled along the dusty road, sitting back in the bed of a pickup, he began to speak very rapidly to me. He was talking about a mountain over there, telling me a story about some wallabies that came to that mountain in the dreamtime and got into some kind of mischief with some lizard girls. He had hardly finished that and he started in on another story about another hill over here and another story over there. I couldn't keep up. I realized after about half an hour of this that these were tales to be told while *walking*, and that I was experiencing a speeded-up version of what might be leisurely told over several days of foot travel. Mr. Tjungurrayi felt graciously compelled to share a body of lore with me by virtue of the simple fact that I was there.

So remember a time when you journeyed on foot over hundreds of miles, walking fast and often traveling at night, traveling nightlong and napping in the acacia shade during the day, and these stories were told to you as you went. In your travels with an older person you were given a map you could memorize, full of lore and song, and also practical information. Off by yourself you could sing those songs to bring yourself back. And you could maybe travel to a place that you'd never been, steering only by songs you had learned.

We made camp at a waterhole called Ilpili and rendezvoused with a number of Pintubi people from the surrounding desert country. The Ilpili waterhole is about a yard across, six inches deep, in a little swale of bush full of finch. People camp a quarter mile away. It's the only waterhole that stays full through drought years in tens of thousands of square miles. A place kept by custom open to all. Until late at night Jimmy and the other old men sat around a small thornbrush fire and sang a cycle of journey songs, walking through a space of desert in imagination and music. They kept a steady rhythmic beat to the song by clapping two boomerangs together. They stopped between songs and would hum a phrase or two and then argue a bit about the words and then start again. One would defer to another and let him start. Jimmy explained to me that they have so many cycles of journey songs they can't quite remember them all, and they have to be constantly rehearsing.

Each night they'd start the evening saying, "What will we sing?" and get a reply like "Let's sing the walk up to Darwin." They'd start out and argue and sing and clap their way along through it. It was during the full moon period: a few clouds would sail and trail in the cool light and mild desert wind. I had learned that the elders liked black tea, and several times a night I'd make a pot right at the fire, with lots of white sugar, the way they wanted it. The singers would stop when they felt like it. I'd ask Jimmy, "How far did you get tonight?" He'd say, "Well, we got two-thirds of the way to Darwin." This can be seen as one example of the many ways landscape, myth, and information were braided together in preliterate societies.

One day driving near Ilpili we stopped the truck and Jimmy and the three other elderly gentlemen got out and he said, "We'll take you to see a sacred place here. I guess you're old enough." They turned to the boys and told them to stay behind. As we climbed the bedrock hill these ordinarily cheery and loud-talking aboriginal men began to drop their voices. As we got higher up they were speaking whispers and their whole manner changed. One said almost inaudibly, "Now we are coming close." Then they got on their hands and knees and crawled. We crawled up the last two hundred feet, then over a little rise into a small basin of broken and oddly shaped rocks. They whispered to us with respect and awe of what was there. Then we all backed away. We got back down the hill and at a certain point stood and walked. At another point voices rose. Back at the truck, everybody was talking loud again and no more mention was made of the sacred place.

Very powerful. Very much in mind. We learned later that it was indeed a place where young men were taken for ceremony.

I traveled by pickup truck along hundreds of miles of rough dirt tracks and hiked into the mountainous and rocky country where the roads stopped. I was being led to special places. There were large unique boulders, each face and facet a surprise. There was the sudden opening out of a hidden steep defile where two cliffs meet with just a little sandbed between, and some green bushes, some parrots calling. We dropped down cliffs off a mesa into a waterhole you wouldn't guess was there, where a thirty-foot blade of rock stands on end, balancing. Each of these spots was out of the ordinary, fantastic even, and sometimes rich with life. Often there were pictographs in the vicinity. They were described as teaching spots and some were "dreaming spots" for certain totem ancestors, well established in song and story over tens of thousands of square miles.

"Dreaming" or "dreamtime" refers to a time of fluidity, shapeshifting, interspecies conversation and intersexuality, radically creative moves, whole landscapes being altered. It is often taken to be a "mythical past," but it is not really in *any* time. We might as well say it is *right now*. It is the mode of the eternal moment of creating, of being, as contrasted with the mode of cause and effect in time. Time is the realm where people mainly live and within which history, evolution, and progress are imagined to take place. Dōgen gave a difficult and playful talk on the resolution of these two modes early in the winter of 1240. It is called "Time/Being."

In Australian lore the totem dreaming place is first of all special to the people of that totem, who sometimes make pilgrimages there. Second, it is sacred (say) to the honey-ants which actually live there—there are hundreds of thousands of them. Third, it's like a little Platonic cave of ideal honey-antness, maybe the creation spot for all honey-ants. It mysteriously connects the essence of honey-antness with the archetypes of the human psyche and makes bridges between humanity, the ants, and the desert. The honey-ant place is in stories, dances, songs, and it is a real place which also happens to be optimum habitat for a world of ants. Or take a green parrot dreaming place: the stories will tell of the tracks of the ancestors going across the landscape and stopping at that dreaming place, and it is truly a perfect place for parrots. All this is a radically different way of expressing what science says, as well as another set of metaphors for the teachings of the Hua-yen or the Avatamsaka Sutra.

This sacredness implies a sense of optimal habitat for certain kinfolk that we have out there—the wallabies, red kangaroo, bush turkeys, lizards. Geoffrey Blainey (1976, 202) says, "The land itself was their chapel and their shrines were hills and creeks and their religious relics were animals, plants, and birds. Thus the migrations of aboriginals, though spurred by economic need, were also always pilgrimages." Good (productive of much life), wild (naturally), and sacred were one.

This way of life, frail and battered as it is, still exists. Now it is threatened by Japanese and other uranium mining projects, large-scale copper mining, and petroleum exploration. The issue of sacredness has become very political—so much so that the Australian Bureau of Aboriginal Affairs has hired some bilingual anthropologists and bush people to work with elders of the different tribes to try and identify sacred sites and map them. There has been much hope

that the Australian government would act in good faith and declare
certain areas off-limits before any exploratory team even gets near
them. This effort is spurred by the fact that there have already been
some confrontations in the Kimberly region over oil exploration, as
at Nincoomba. The local native people stood their ground, making
human lines in front of bulldozers and drilling rigs, and the media
coverage of this resistance won over some of the Australian public.
Since in Australia a landowner's mineral rights are always reserved to
"The Crown," even somebody's ranch might be subject to mining.
So to consider sacred land a special category, even in theory, is an advanced move. But it's shaky. A "registered site" near Alice Springs
was bulldozed supposedly on the instructions of a government land
minister, and this was in the relatively benign federal jurisdiction!

Shrines

The original inhabitants of Japan, the Ainu, had a way of speaking
of the sacredness and specialness of a whole ecosystem. Their term
iworu means "field" with implications of watershed region, plant
and animal communities, and spirit force—the powers behind the
masks or armor, *hayakpe*, of the various beings. The *iworu* of the
Great Brown Bear would be the mountain habitat—and connected
lowland valley system—in which the bear is dominant, and it would
mean the myth and spirit world of the bear as well. The *iworu* of
salmon would be the lower watersheds with all their tributaries (and
the associated plant communities), and on out to sea, extending into
oceanic realms only guessed at, where the salmon do their weaving.
The bear field, the deer field, the salmon field, the Orca field.

In the Ainu world a few human houses are in a valley by a little
river. The doorways all face east. In the center of each house is the
firepit. The sunshine streams through the eastern door each morning to touch the fire, and they say the sun goddess is visiting her sister the fire goddess in the firepit. One should not walk through sun-

beams that shine on the fire—that would be breaking their contact. Food is often foraged in the local area, but some of the creatures come down from the inner mountains and up from the deeps of the sea. The animal or fish (or plant) that allows itself to be killed or gathered, and then enters the house to be consumed, is called a "visitor," *marapto*.

The master of the sea is Orca, the Killer Whale; the master of the inner mountains is Bear. Bear sends his friends the deer down to visit humans. Orca sends his friends the salmon up the streams. When they arrive their "armor is broken"—they are killed—enabling them to shake off their fur or scale coats and step out as invisible spirit beings. They are then delighted by witnessing the human entertainments—saké and music. (They love music.) The people sing songs to them and eat their flesh. Having enjoyed their visit they return to the deep sea or to the inner mountains and report: "We had a wonderful time with the human beings." The others are then prompted themselves to go on visits. Thus if the humans do not neglect proper hospitality—music and manners—when entertaining their deer or salmon or wild plant *marapto*, the beings will be reborn and return over and over. This is a sort of spiritual game management.

Modern Japan is another sort of example: a successful industrialized country with remnants of sacred landscape consciousness still intact. There are Shinto shrines throughout the Japanese islands. Shinto is "the way of the spirits." *Kami* are a formless "power" present in everything to some degree but intensified in strength and presence in certain outstanding objects such as large curiously twisted boulders, very old trees, or thundering misty waterfalls. Anomalies and curiosities of the landscape are all signs of *kami*—spirit-power, presence, shape of mind, energy. The greatest of *kami* centers is Mt. Fuji. The name Fuji is now thought to derive from that of the Ainu Fire Goddess, the only one who stands above and can scold and correct the *kimun kamui*, mountain deity, Bear. All of Mt. Fuji is a Shinto shrine, the largest in the nation, from well below timberline all the way to the summit. (Many place names left behind by the displaced Ainu are still current in Japan.)

Shinto got a bad name during the 1930s and World War II because the Japanese had created an artificial "State Shinto" in the service of militarism and nationalism. It and folk Shinto became confused in the minds of many Euro-Americans. Long before the rise of any state, the islands of Japan were studded with little shrines— *jinja* and *omiya*—that were part of neolithic village culture. Even in the midst of the onrushing industrial energy of the current system, shrine lands still remain untouchable. It would make your hair stand up to see how a Japanese developer will take bulldozers to a nice slope of old pines and level it for a new town. When the New Island was created in Kobe harbor to make Kobe the second busiest port in the world (after Rotterdam), it was raised from the bay bottom with dirt obtained by shaving down a whole range of hills ten miles south of the city. This was barged to the site for twelve years—a steady stream of barges carrying dirt off giant conveyor belts that totally removed soil two rows of hills back from the coast. The newly leveled area became a housing development. In industrial Japan it's not that "nothing is sacred," it's that the *sacred* is sacred and that's *all* that's sacred.

We are grateful for these microscopic traces of salvaged land in Japan because the rule in shrines is that (away from the buildings and paths) you never cut anything, never maintain anything, never clear or thin anything. No hunting, no fishing, no thinning, no burning, no stopping of burning: leaving us a very few stands of ancient forests right inside the cities. One can walk into a little *jinja* and be in the presence of an 800-year-old Cryptomeria (*Sugi*) tree. Without the shrines we wouldn't know so well what the original Japanese forest might have been. But such compartmentalization is not healthy: in this patriarchal model some land is saved, like a virgin priestess, some is overworked endlessly, like a wife, and some is brutally publicly reshaped, like an exuberant girl declared promiscuous and punished. Good, wild, and sacred couldn't be farther apart.

Europe and the Middle East were once studded with similar shrines. They were even spoken of as "sacred groves." It may be that in the remote past the most sacred spot in all of Europe was under the Pyrenees, where the great cave paintings are. I suspect they were part of a religious center thirty thousand years ago, where animals were "conceived" underground. Perhaps a dreaming place. Maybe a thought that the animals' secret hearts were thereby hidden under the earth, a way of keeping them from becoming extinct. But many species did become extinct, some even before the era of cave paintings was over. Many more have become so during the last two thousand years, victims of civilization. Occidental expansion brought an acceleration of habitat degradation to the whole globe, but it is interesting to note that even before that expansion such political and economic processes were already well under way. The destruction of species, the impoverishment and enslavement of rural people, and the persecution of nature-worship traditions has long been part of Europe.

So the French and English explorers of North America, the early fur traders, had no teachings from the societies they left behind that would urge them to look on wild nature with reverence. They did find much that was awe-inspiring, and some expressed it well. Some even joined the Indians and became people of the New World. These few almost forgotten exceptions were overwhelmed by trading entrepreneurs and, later, settlers. Yet all through American history there were some who kept joining the Indians in fact or in style—and some, even in the eighteenth century, who realized that the world they saw would shrink away. In the Far East, or Europe, the notion of an ancient forest or original prairie and all the splendid creatures that might live there is now a tale told from the neolithic.

In the western United States it was the world of our grandmothers. For many of us today this loss is a source of grief. For Native Americans this was a loss of land, traditional life, and the sources of their culture.

True Nature

Thoreau set out to "make the soil say beans" while living by his pond. To cause land to be productive according to our own notion is not evil. But we must also ask: what does mother nature do best when left to her own long strategies? This comes to asking what the full potential vegetation of a spot would be. For all land, however wasted and exploited, if left to nature (*zi-ran*, the self-so), will arrive at a point of balance between biological productivity and stability. A sophisticated postindustrial "future primitive" agriculture will be asking: is there any way we can go *with* rather than against nature's tendency? Go toward, say, in New England, deciduous hardwoods—or, as where I live, a mix of pine and oak with kitkitdizze ground cover? Doing horticulture, agriculture, or forestry with the grain rather than against it would be in the human interest and not just for the long run.

Wes Jackson's research suggests that a diverse and perennial-plant-based agriculture holds real promise for sustaining the locally appropriate communities of the future. This is acknowledging that the source of fertility ultimately is the "wild." It has been said that "good soil is good because of the wildness in it." How could *this* be granted by a victorious king dividing up his spoils? The fatuity of "Spanish land grants" and "Real Estate." The power that gives us good land is none other than Gaia herself, the whole network. It might be that almost all civilized agriculture has been on the wrong path from the beginning, relying as it does on the monoculture of annuals. In *New Roots for Agriculture* Wes Jackson develops this argument. I concur with his view, knowing that it raises even larger questions about civilization itself, a critique I have worked at else-where. Suffice it to say that the sorts of economic and social organi-zation we invoke when we say "civilization" can no longer be auto-matically accepted as useful models. To scrutinize civilization is not, however, to negate all the meanings of cultivation.

The word *cultivation*, harking to etymologies of *till* and *wheel about*, generally implies a movement away from natural process. In agriculture it is a matter of "arresting succession, establishing monoculture." Applied on the spiritual plane this has meant auster-ities, obedience to religious authority, long bookish scholarship, or in some traditions a dualistic devotionalism (sharply distinguishing "creature" and "creator") and an overriding image of divinity being "centralized," a distant and singular point of perfection to aim at. The efforts entailed in such a spiritual practice are sometimes a sort of war against nature—placing the human over the animal and the spiritual over the human. The most sophisticated modern variety of hierarchical spirituality is the work of Father Teilhard de Chardin, who claims a special evolutionary spiritual destiny for humanity un-der the name of higher consciousness. Some of the most extreme of these Spiritual Darwinists would willingly leave the rest of earth-bound animal and plant life behind to enter an off-the-planet realm transcending biology. The anthropocentrism of some new age thinkers is countered by the radical critique of the Deep Ecology movement.

On the social level cultivation has meant the absorption of lan-guage, lore, and manners that guarantee membership in the elite class and is to be contrasted with "vernacular manners." The truth is, of course, that the etiquette of villagers or nomads (Charles Doughty having black coffee with his Bedouin hosts in Arabia De-serta) can be as elaborate, complex, and arbitrary as that of any city-dweller.

Yet there is such a thing as training. The world moves by comple-mentaries of young and old, foolish and wise, ripe or green, raw or cooked. Animals too learn self-discipline and caution in the face of desire and availability. There is learning and training that goes *with* the grain of things as well as against it. In early Chinese Daoism, "training" did not mean to cultivate the wildness out of oneself, but to do away with arbitrary and delusive conditioning. Zhuang-zi seems to be saying that all social values are false and generate self-serving ego. Buddhism takes a middle path—allowing that greed, hatred, and ignorance are intrinsic to ego, but that ego itself is a reflex of ignorance and delusion that comes from not seeing who we "truly" are. Organized society can inflame, pander to, or exploit these weaknesses, or it can encourage generosity, kindness, trust. There is reason, therefore, to be engaged in a politics of virtue. Still it is a matter of individual character as to whether or not one makes a little private vow to work for compassion and insight or overlooks this possibility. The day-to-day actualization of the vow calls for practice: for a training that helps us realize our own true nature, and nature.

Greed exposes the foolish person or the foolish chicken alike to the ever-watchful hawk of the food-web and to early impermanence. Preliterate hunting and gathering cultures were highly trained and lived well by virtue of keen observation and good manners; as noted earlier, stinginess was the worst of vices. We also know that early economies often were more manipulative of the environment than is commonly realized. The people of mesolithic Britain selectively cleared or burned in the valley of the Thames as a way to encourage the growth of hazel. An almost invisible system of nut and fruit tree growing was once practiced in the jungles of Guatemala. A certain kind of training and culture can be grounded in the wild.

We can all agree: there is a problem with the self-seeking human ego. Is it a mirror of the wild and of nature? I think not: for civilization itself is ego gone to seed and institutionalized in the form of the State, both Eastern and Western. It is not nature-as-chaos which threatens us, but the State's presumption that *it* has created order.

Also there is an almost self-congratulatory *ignorance* of the natural world that is pervasive in Euro-American business, political, and religious circles. Nature is orderly. That which appears to be chaotic in nature is only a more complex kind of order.

Now we can rethink what sacred land might be. For a people of an old culture, *all* their mutually owned territory holds numinous life and spirit. Certain places are perceived to be of high spiritual density because of plant or animal habitat intensities, or associations with legend, or connections with human totemic ancestry, or because of geomorphological anomaly, or some combination of qualities. These places are gates through which one can—it would be said—more easily be touched by a larger-than-human, larger-than-personal, view.

Concern for the environment and the fate of the earth is spreading over the world. In Asia environmentalism is perceived foremost as a movement concerned with health—and seeing the condition of their air and water, this is to be expected. In the Western Hemisphere we have similar problems. But here we are blessed with a bit of remaining wilderness, a heritage to be preserved for all the people of the world. In the Western Hemisphere we have only the tiniest number of buildings that can be called temples or shrines. The temples of our hemisphere will be some of the planet's remaining wilderness areas. When we enter them on foot we can sense that the *kami* or (Maidu) *kukini* are still in force here. They have become the refuge of the Mountain Lions, Mountain Sheep, and Grizzlies—three North American animals which were found throughout the lower hills and plains in prewhite times. The rocky icy grandeur of the high country—and the rich shadowy bird and fish-streaked southern swamps—remind us of the overarching wild systems that nourish us all and underwrite the industrial economy. In the sterile beauty of mountain snowfields and glaciers begin the little streams that water the agribusiness fields of the great Central Valley of Cal-

ifornia. The wilderness pilgrim's step-by-step breath-by-breath
walk up a trail, into those snowfields, carrying all on the back, is so
ancient a set of gestures as to bring a profound sense of body-mind
joy.

Not just backpackers, of course. The same happens to those who
sail in the ocean, kayak fjords or rivers, tend a garden, peel garlic,
even sit on a meditation cushion. The point is to make intimate contact with the real world, real self. *Sacred* refers to that which helps
take us (not only human beings) out of our little selves into the whole
mountains-and-rivers mandala universe. Inspiration, exaltation,
and insight do not end when one steps outside the doors of the
church. The wilderness as a temple is only a beginning. One should
not dwell in the specialness of the extraordinary experience nor hope
to leave the political quagg behind to enter a perpetual state of
heightened insight. The best purpose of such studies and hikes is to
be able to come back to the lowlands and see all the land about us,
agricultural, suburban, urban, as part of the same territory—never
totally ruined, never completely unnatural. It can be restored, and
humans could live in considerable numbers on much of it. Great
Brown Bear is walking with us, Salmon swimming upstream with
us, as we stroll a city street.

To return to my own situation: the land my family and I live on in the
Sierra Nevada of California is "barely good" from an economic
standpoint. With soil amendments, much labor, and the development of ponds for holding water through the dry season, it is pro-
ducing a few vegetables and some good apples. It is better as forest:
through the millennia it has excelled at growing oak and pine. I
guess I should admit that it's better left wild. Most of it is being
"managed for wild" right now—the pines are getting large and
some of the oaks were growing here before a Euro-American set foot
anywhere in California. The deer and all the other animals move
through with the exception of Grizzly Bear and wolf; they are tem-

porarily not in residence in California. We will someday bring them back.

These foothill ridges are not striking in any special way, no post-card scenery, but the deer are so at home here I think it might be a "deer field." And the fact that my neighbors and I and all of our children have learned so much by taking our place in these Sierra foot-hills—logged-over land now come back, burned-over land recover-ing, considered worthless for decades—begins to make this land a teacher to us. It is the place on earth we work with, struggle with, and where we stick out the summers and winters. It has shown us a little of its beauty.

And sacred? One could indulge in a bit of woo-woo and say, yes, there are newly discovered sacred places in our reinhabited land-scape. I know my children (like kids everywhere) have some secret spots in the woods. There is a local hill where many people walk for the view, the broad night sky, moon-viewing, and to blow a conch at dawn on Bodhi Day. There are miles of mined-over gravels where we have held ceremonies to apologize for the stripping of trees and soil and to help speed the plant-succession recovery. There are some deep groves where people got married.

Even this much connection with the place is enough to inspire the local community to hold on: renewed gold mining and stepped-up logging press in on us. People volunteer to be on committees to study the mining proposals, critique the environmental impact re-ports, challenge the sloppy assumptions of the corporations, and stand up to certain county officials who would sell out the inhabi-tants and hand over the whole area to any glamorous project. It is hard, unpaid, frustrating work for people who already have to work full time to support their families. The same work goes on with for-estry issues—exposing the scandalous favoritism shown the timber industry by our nearby national forest, as its managers try to pacify the public with sweet words and frivolous statistics. Any lightly populated area with "resources" is exploited like a Third World country, even within the United States. We are defending our own space, and we are trying to protect the commons. More than the logic of self-interest inspires this: a true and selfless love of the land is the source of the undaunted spirit of my neighbors.

There's no rush about calling things sacred. I think we should be patient, and give the land a lot of time to tell us or the people of the future. The cry of a Flicker, the funny urgent chatter of a Gray Squirrel, the acorn whack on a barn roof—are signs enough.

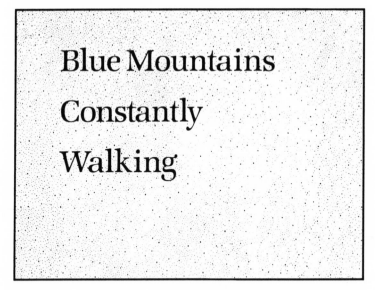

Blue Mountains Constantly Walking

Fudō and Kannon

> The mountains and rivers of this moment are the actualization of the way of the ancient Buddhas. Each, abiding in its own phenomenal expression, realizes completeness. Because mountains and waters have been active since before the eon of emptiness, they are alive at this moment. Because they have been the self since before form arose, they are liberated and realized.

This is the opening paragraph of Dōgen Kigen's astonishing essay *Sansuikyo*, "Mountains and Waters Sutra," written in the autumn of 1240, thirteen years after he returned from his visit to Song-dynasty China. At the age of twelve he had left home in Kyoto to climb the well-worn trails through the dark hinoki and sugi (cedar-and-sequoia-like) forests of Mt. Hiei. This three-thousand-foot range at the northeast corner of the Kamo River basin, the broad valley now occupied by the huge city of Kyoto, was the Japanese headquarters mountain of the Tendai sect of Buddhism. He became a novice monk in one of the red-painted shadowy wooden temples along the ridges.

"The blue mountains are constantly walking."

In those days travelers walked. The head monk at the Daitoku-ji Zen monks' hall in Kyoto once showed me the monastery's handwritten "Yearly Tasks" book from the nineteenth century. (It had been replaced by another handwritten volume with a few minor updates for the twentieth century.) These are the records that the leaders refer to through the year in keeping track of ceremonies, meditation sessions, and recipes. It listed the temples that were affiliated with this training school in order of the traveling time it took to get to them: from one day to four weeks' walk. Student monks from even those distant temples usually made a round trip home at least once a year.

Virtually all of Japan is steep hills and mountains dissected by fast shallow streams that open into shoestring valleys and a few wider river plains toward the sea. The hills are generally covered with small conifers and shrubs. Once they were densely forested with a cover of large hardwoods as well as the irregular pines and the tall straight hinoki and sugi. Traces of a vast network of well-marked trails are still found throughout the land. They were tramped down by musicians, monks, merchants, porters, pilgrims, and periodic armies.

We learn a place and how to visualize spatial relationships, as children, on foot and with imagination. Place and the scale of space must be measured against our bodies and their capabilities. A "mile" was originally a Roman measure of one thousand paces. Automobile and airplane travel teaches us little that we can easily translate into a perception of space. To know that it takes six months to walk across Turtle Island/North America walking steadily but comfortably all day every day is to get some grasp of the distance. The Chinese spoke of the "four dignities"—Standing, Lying, Sitting, and Walking. They are "dignities" in that they are ways of being fully ourselves, at home in our bodies, in their fundamental modes. I think many of us would consider it quite marvelous if we could set out on foot again, with a little inn or a clean camp available every ten or so miles and no threat from traffic, to travel across a large landscape—all of China, all of Europe. That's the way to see the world: in our own bodies.

Sacred mountains and pilgrimage to them is a deeply established feature of the popular religions of Asia. When Dōgen speaks of mountains he is well aware of these prior traditions. There are hundreds of famous Daoist and Buddhist peaks in China and similar Buddhist and Shinto-associated mountains in Japan. There are several sorts of sacred mountains in Asia: a "sacred site" that is the residence of a spirit or deity is the simplest and possibly oldest. Then there are "sacred areas"—perhaps many dozens of square miles—that are special to the mythology and practice of a sect with its own set of Daoist or Buddhist deities—miles of paths—and dozens or hundreds of little temples and shrines. Pilgrims might climb thousands of feet, sleep in the plain board guesthouses, eat rice gruel and a few pickles, and circumambulate set routes burning incense and bowing at site after site.

Finally there are a few highly formalized sacred areas that have been deliberately modeled on a symbolic diagram (mandala) or a holy text. They too can be quite large. It is thought that to walk within the designated landscape is to enact specific moves on the spiritual plane (Grapard, 1982). Some friends and I once walked the ancient pilgrimage route of the Ōmine Yamabushi (mountain ascetics) in Nara prefecture from Yoshino to Kumano. In doing so we crossed the traditional center of the "Diamond-Realm Mandala" at the summit of Mt. Ōmine (close to six thousand feet) and four hiking days later descended to the center of the "Womb-Realm Mandala" at the Kumano ("Bear Field") Shrine, deep in a valley. It was the late-June rainy season, flowery and misty. There were little stone shrines the whole distance—miles of ridges—to which we sincerely bowed each time we came on them. This projection of complex teaching diagrams onto the landscape comes from the Japanese variety of Vajrayana Buddhism, the Shingon sect, in its interaction with the shamanistic tradition of the mountain brotherhood.

The regular pilgrimage up Mt. Ōmine from the Yoshino side is flourishing—hundreds of colorful Yamabushi in medieval mountain-gear scale cliffs, climb the peak, and blow conches while others chant sutras in the smoky dirt-floored temple on the summit. The long-distance practice has been abandoned in recent years, so the trail was so overgrown it was almost impossible to find. This four-thousand-foot-high direct ridge route makes excellent sense, and I suspect it was the regular way of traveling from the coast to the interior in paleolithic and neolithic times. It was the only place I ever came on wild deer and monkeys in Japan.

In East Asia "mountains" are often synonymous with wilderness. The agrarian states have long since drained, irrigated, and terraced the lowlands. Forest and wild habitat start at the very place the farming stops. The lowlands, with their villages, markets, cities, palaces, and wineshops, are thought of as the place of greed, lust, competition, commerce, and intoxication—the "dusty world." Those who would flee such a world and seek purity find caves or build hermitages in the hills—and take up the practices which will bring realization or at least a long healthy life. These hermitages in time became the centers of temple complexes and ultimately religious sects. Dōgen says:

> Many rulers have visited mountains to pay homage to wise people or ask for instructions from great sages. . . . At such time these rulers treat the sages as teachers, disregarding the protocol of the usual world. The imperial power has no authority over the wise people in the mountains.

So "mountains" are not only spiritually deepening but also (it is hoped) independent of the control of the central government. Joining the hermits and priests in the hills are people fleeing jail, taxes, or conscription. (Deeper into the ranges of southwestern China are the surviving hill tribes who worship dogs and tigers and have much equality between the sexes, but that belongs to another story.) Mountains (or wilderness) have served as a haven of spiritual and political freedom all over.

Mountains also have mythic associations of verticality, spirit, height, transcendence, hardness, resistance, and masculinity. For the Chinese they are exemplars of the "yang": dry, hard, male, and bright. Waters are feminine: wet, soft, dark "yin" with associations of fluid-but-strong, seeking (and carving) the lowest, soulful, life-giving, shape-shifting. Folk (and Vajrayana) Buddhist iconography personifies "mountains and waters" in the *rupas*—"images" of Fudō Myō-ō (Immovable Wisdom King) and Kannon Bosatsu (The Bodhisattva Who Watches the Waves). Fudō is almost comically ferocious-looking with a blind eye and a fang, seated or standing on a slab of rock and enveloped in flames. He is known as an ally of mountain ascetics. Kannon (Kuan-yin, Avalokitesvara) gracefully leans forward with her lotus and vase of water, a figure of compassion. The two are seen as buddha-work partners: ascetic discipline and relentless spirituality balanced by compassionate tolerance and detached forgiveness. Mountains and Waters are a dyad that together make wholeness possible: wisdom and compassion are the two components of realization. Dōgen says:

> Wenzi said, "The path of water is such that when it rises to the sky, it becomes raindrops; when it falls to the ground, it becomes rivers."
> . . . The path of water is not noticed by water, but is realized by water.

There is the obvious fact of the water-cycle and the fact that mountains and rivers indeed form each other: waters are precipitated by heights, carve or deposit landforms in their flowing descent, and weight the offshore continental shelves with sediment to ultimately tilt more uplifts. In common usage the compound "mountains and waters"—*shan-shui* in Chinese—is the straightforward term for landscape. Landscape painting is "mountains and waters pictures." (A mountain range is sometimes also termed *mai*, a "pulse" or "vein"—as a network of veins on the back of a hand.) One does not need to be a specialist to observe that landforms are a play of stream-cutting and ridge-resistance and that waters and hills interpenetrate in endlessly branching rhythms. The Chinese feel for land has always incorporated this sense of a dialectic of rock and water, of downward flow and rocky uplift, and of the dynamism and "slow flowing" of earth-forms. There are several surviving large Chinese horizontal handscrolls from premodern eras titled something like "Mountains and Rivers Without End." Some of them move through the four seasons and seem to picture the whole world.

"Mountains and waters" is a way to refer to the totality of the process of nature. As such it goes well beyond dichotomies of purity and pollution, natural and artificial. The whole, with its rivers and valleys, obviously includes farms, fields, villages, cities, and the (once comparatively small) dusty world of human affairs.

This

>"The blue mountains are constantly walking."

Dōgen is quoting the Chan master Furong. Dōgen was probably envisioning those mountains of Asia whose trails he had walked over the years—peaks in the three to nine-thousand-foot range, hazy blue or blue-green, mostly tree-covered, maybe the steep jumbled mountains of coastal South China where he had lived and practiced thirteen years earlier. (Timberline at these latitudes is close to nine thousand feet—none of these are alpine mountains.) He had walked thousands of miles. ("The Mind studies the way running barefoot.")

> If you doubt mountains walking you do not know your own walking.

Dōgen is not concerned with "sacred mountains"—or pilgrimages, or spirit allies, or wilderness as some special quality. His mountains and streams are the processes of this earth, all of existence, process, essence, action, absence; they roll being and nonbeing together. They are what we are, we are what they are. For those who would see directly into essential nature, the idea of the sacred is a delusion and an obstruction: it diverts us from seeing what is before our eyes: plain thusness. Roots, stems, and branches are all equally scratchy. No hierarchy, no equality. No occult and exoteric, no gifted kids and slow achievers. No wild and tame, no bound or free, no natural and artificial. Each totally its own frail self. Even though connected all which ways; even *because* connected all which ways.

This, *thusness*, is the nature of the nature of nature. The wild in wild.

So the blue mountains walk to the kitchen and back to the shop, to the desk, to the stove. We sit on the park bench and let the wind and rain drench us. The blue mountains walk out to put another coin in the parking meter, and go on down to the 7-Eleven. The blue mountains march out of the sea, shoulder the sky for a while, and slip back into the waters.

Homeless

The Buddhists say "homeless" to mean a monk or priest. (In Japanese, *shukke*—literally "out of the house.") It refers to a person who has supposedly left the householder's life and the temptations and

obligations of the secular world behind. Another phrase, "leaving
the world," means getting away from the imperfections of human
behavior—particularly as reinforced by urban life. It does not mean
distancing yourself from the natural world. For some it has meant
living as mountain hermits or members of religious communities.
The "house" has been set against "mountains" or "purity." Enlarg-
ing the scale of the homeless world the fifth-century poet Zhiang-
yan said the proper hermit should "take the purple heavens to be his
hut, the encircling sea to be his pond, roaring with laughter in his
nakedness, walking along singing with his hair hanging down"
(Watson, 1971, 82). The early Tang poet Han-shan is taken as the
veritable model of a recluse—his spacious home reaches to the end
of the universe:

> I settled at Cold Mountain long ago,
> Already it seems like years and years.
> Freely drifting, I prowl the woods and streams
> And linger watching things themselves.
> Men don't get this far into the mountains,
> White clouds gather and billow.
> Thin grass does for a mattress,
> The blue sky makes a good quilt.
> Happy with a stone underhead
> Let heaven and earth go about their changes.

"Homeless" is here coming to mean "being at home in the whole universe." In a similar way, self-determining people who have not lost
the wholeness of their place can see their households and their regional mountains or woods as within the same sphere.

   I attended the ceremonies at the shrine for the volcanic mountain
of Suwa-no-se Island, in the East China Sea, one year. The path
through the jungle needed brushing, so rarely did people go there.
Two of us from the Banyan Ashram went as helpers to three elders.
We spent the morning cutting overgrowth back, sweeping the

ground, opening and wiping the unpainted wood altar-structure (about the size of a pigeon coop), and then placing some offerings of sweet potatoes, fruit, and *shochu* on the shelf before the blank space that in fact framed the mountain itself. One elder then faced the peak (which had been belching out ash clouds lately) and made a direct, perfunctory personal speech or prayer in dialect. We sat on the ground sweating and cut open watermelon with a sickle and drank some of the strong *shochu* then, while the old guys told stories of other days in the islands. Tall thick glossy green trees arched over us, roaring with cicada. It was not trivial. The domestic parallel is accomplished in each household with its photos of ancestors, offerings of rice and alcohol, and a vase with a few twigs of wild evergreen leaves. The house itself, with its funky tiny kitchen, bath, well, and entranceway altars, becomes a little shrine.

And then the literal "house," when seen as just another piece of the world, is itself impermanent and composite, a poor "homeless" thing in its own right. Houses are made up, heaped together, of pine boards, clay tiles, cedar battens, river boulder piers, windows scrounged from wrecking yards, knobs from K-Mart, mats from Cost Plus, kitchen floor of sandstone from some mountain ridge, doormat from Longs—made up of the same world as you and me and mice.

> Blue mountains are neither sentient nor insentient. You are neither sentient nor insentient. At this moment, you cannot doubt the blue mountains walking.

Not only plum blossoms and clouds, or Lecturers and Rōshis, but chisels, bent nails, wheelbarrows, and squeaky doors are all teaching the truth of the way things are. The condition of true "homelessness" is the maturity of relying on nothing and responding to whatever turns up on the doorstep. Dōgen encourages us with "A mountain always practices in every place."

Larger Than a Wolf, Smaller Than an Elk

All my life I have been in and around wild nature, working, exploring, studying, even while living in cities. Yet I realized a few years ago that I had never made myself into as good a botanist or zoologist or ornithologist as so many of the outdoor people I admire have done. Recalling where I had put my intellectual energies over the years it came to me that I had made my fellow human beings my study—that I had been a naturalist of my own species. I had been my own object-of-study too. I enjoy learning how different societies work out the details of subsistence and celebration in their different landscapes. Science, technology, and the economic uses of nature need not be antithetical to celebration. The line between use and misuse, between objectification and celebration, is fine indeed.

The line is in the details. I once attended the dedication of a Japanese temple building that had been broken down and transported across the Pacific to be resurrected on the West Coast. The dedication ceremony was in the Shinto style and included offerings of flowers and plants. The difficulty was that they were the plants that would have been used in a traditional Japanese dedication and had been sent from Japan—they were not plants of the new place. The ritualists had the forms right but clearly didn't grasp the substance. After everyone had gone home I tried to make brief introductions myself: "Japanese building of hinoki wood, meet manzanita and Ponderosa Pine . . . please take care of yourself in this dry climate. Manzanita, this building is used to damp air and lots of people. Please accept it in place of your dusty slopes." Humans provide their own sort of access to understanding nature and the wild.

The human diverseness of style and costume, and the constant transformations of popular culture, is a kind of symbolic speciation—as though humans chose to mimic the colors and patterns of birds. People from the high civilizations in particular have elaborate notions of separateness and difference and dozens of ways to declare themselves "out of nature." As a kind of game this might be harmless. (One could imagine the phylum Chordata declaring, "We are a qualitative leap in evolution representing something entirely transcendent entering what has hitherto been merely biology.") But at the very minimum this call to a special destiny on the part of human beings can be seen as a case of needlessly multiplying theories (Occam's razor). And the results—in the human treatment of the rest of nature—have been pernicious.

There is a large landscape handscroll called "Interminable Mountains and Streams" (attributed to Lu Yuan of the Ching dynasty; now in the Freer). We see, within this larger scope of rocks, trees, ridges, mountains, and watercourses, people and their works. There are peasants and thatched huts, priests and complexes of temples, scholars at their little windows, fishermen in their boats, traveling merchants with their loads, matrons, children. While the Buddhist tradition of North India and Tibet made the mandala—painted or drawn charts of the positions of consciousness and cause-and-effect chains—their visual teaching aids, the Chan tradition of China (especially the Southern Song) did something similar (I will venture to suggest) with landscape painting. If a scroll is taken as a kind of Chinese mandala, then all the characters in it are our various little selves, and the cliffs, trees, waterfalls, and clouds are our own changes and stations. (Swampy reedy thicket along a stream—what does *that* say?) Each type of ecological system is a different mandala, a different imagination. Again the Ainu term *iworu*, field-of-beings, comes to mind.

> All beings do not see mountains and waters in the same way. . . .
> Some see water as wondrous blossoms, hungry ghosts see water as
> raging fire or pus and blood. Dragons see water as a palace or a pavil-
> ion. . . . Some beings see water as a forest or a wall. Human beings
> see water as water. . . . Water's freedom depends only on water.

One July walking down from the headwaters of the Koyukuk River in the Brooks Range of Alaska I found myself able to look into the realm of Dall (mountain) Sheep. The green cloudy tundra summer alps—in which I was a frail visitor—were the most hospitable they would ever be to a hairless primate. The long dark winters do not daunt the Dall Sheep, though—they do not even migrate down. The winds blow the scant loose snow, and the dried forbs and grasses of arctic summer are nibbled through the year. The dozens of summer sheep stood out white against green: playing, napping, eating, butting, circling, sitting, dozing in their high smoothed out beds on ledges at the "cliff-edge of life and death." Dall Sheep (in Athapaskan called *dibee*) see mountains—Dōgen might say—"as a palace or pavilion." But that provisional phrase "palace or pavilion" is too high-class, urban, and human to really show how totally and uniquely *at home* each life-form must be in its own unique "buddha-field."

> Green mountain walls in blowing cloud
> white dots on far slopes, constellations,
> slowly changing, not stars, not rocks
> "by the midnight breezes strewn"
> cloud tatters, lavender arctic light
> on sedate wild sheep grazing
> tundra greens, held in the web of clan
> and kin by bleats and smells to the slow
> rotation of their Order living
> half in the sky—damp wind up from the
> whole North Slope and a taste of the icepack,
> the primus roaring now,
> here, have some tea.

And down in the little arctic river below the slopes the Grayling with their iridescent bodies are in their own (to us) icy paradise. Dōgen again:

> Now when dragons and fish see water as a palace, it is just like human
> beings seeing a palace. They do not think it flows. If an outsider tells

them, "What you see as a palace is running water," the dragons and fish will be astonished, just as we are when we hear the words, "Mountains flow."

We can begin to imagine, to visualize, the nested hierarchies and webs of the actual nondualistic world. Systems theory provides equations but few metaphors. In the "Mountains and Waters Sutra" we find:

> It is not only that there is water in the world, but there is a world in water. It is not just in water. There is a world of sentient beings in clouds. There is a world of sentient beings in the air. There is a world of sentient beings in fire. . . . There is a world of sentient beings in a blade of grass.

It would appear that the common conception of evolution is that of competing species running a sort of race through time on planet earth, all on the same running field, some dropping out, some flagging, some victoriously in front. If the background and foreground are reversed, and we look at it from the side of the "conditions" and their creative possibilities, we can see these multitudes of interactions through hundreds of other eyes. We could say a food brings a form into existence. Huckleberries and salmon call for bears, the clouds of plankton of the North Pacific call for salmon, and salmon call for seals and thus orcas. The Sperm Whale is sucked into existence by the pulsing, fluctuating pastures of squid, and the open niches of the Galápagos Islands sucked a diversity of bird forms and functions out of one line of finch.

Conservation biologists speak of "indicator species"—animals or birds that are so typical of a natural area and its system that their condition is an indicator of the condition of the whole. The old conifer forests can be measured by "Spotted Owl," and the Great Plains once said (and would say it again) "bison." So the question I have been asking myself is: what says "humans"? What sucks *our* lineage into form? It is surely the "mountains and rivers without end"—the whole of this earth on which we find ourselves more or less competently at home. Berries, acorns, grass-seeds, apples, and yams call for dextrous creatures something like us to come forward. Larger than a wolf, smaller than an elk, human beings are not such huge figures in the landscape. From the air, the works of humanity are scratches and grids and ponds, and in fact most of the earth seems, from afar, to be open land. (We know now that our impact is far greater than it appears.)

As for towns and cities—they are (to those who can see) old tree trunks, riverbed gravels, oil seeps, landslide scrapes, blowdowns and burns, the leavings after floods, coral colonies, paper-wasp nests, beehives, rotting logs, watercourses, rock-cleavage lines, ledge strata layers, guano heaps, feeding frenzies, courting and strutting bowers, lookout rocks, and ground-squirrel apartments. And for a few people they are also palaces.

Decomposed

"Hungry ghosts see water as raging fire or pus and blood . . ."

Life in the wild is not just eating berries in the sunlight. I like to imagine a "depth ecology" that would go to the dark side of nature—the ball of crunched bones in a scat, the feathers in the snow, the tales of insatiable appetite. Wild systems are in one elevated sense above criticism, but they can also be seen as irrational, moldy, cruel, parasitic. Jim Dodge told me how he had watched—with fascinated horror—Orcas methodically batter a Gray Whale to death in the Chukchi Sea. Life is not just a diurnal property of large interesting vertebrates; it is also nocturnal, anaerobic, cannibalistic, microscopic, digestive, fermentative: cooking away in the warm dark. Life is well maintained at a four-mile ocean depth, is waiting and sustained on a frozen rock wall, is clinging and nourished in hundred-degree desert temperatures. And there is a world of nature on the decay side, a world of beings who do rot and decay in the shade. Human beings have made much of purity and are repelled by blood, pollution, putrefaction. The other side of the "sacred" is the sight of your beloved in the underworld, dripping with maggots. Coyote, Orpheus, and Izanagi cannot help but look, and they lose her. Shame, grief, embarrassment, and fear are the anaerobic fuels of the dark imagination. The less familiar energies of the wild world, and their analogs in the imagination, have given us ecologies of the mind.

Here we encounter the peculiar habitat needs of the gods. They settle on the summits of mountains (as on Mt. Olympus), have chambers deep below the earth, or are invisibly all around us. (One major deity is rumored to be domiciled entirely off this earth.) The Yana said that Mt. Lassen of northern California—"Waganupa" in Ishi's tongue, a ten-thousand-foot volcano—is home to countless *kukini* who keep a fire going inside. (The smoke passes out through the smoke-hole.) They will enjoy their magical stick-game gambling until the time that human beings reform themselves and become "real people" that spirits might want to associate with once again.

The spirit world goes across and between species. It does not need to concern itself with reproduction, it is not afraid of death, it is not practical. But the spirits do seem to have an ambivalent, selective interest in cross-world communication. Young women in scarlet and white robes dance to call down the gods, to be possessed by them, to speak in their voices. The priests who employ them can only wait for the message. (I think it was D. H. Lawrence who said, "Drink and carouse with Bacchus, or eat dry bread with Jesus, but don't sit down without one of the gods.")

(The *personal* quality of mountain dreaming: I was half asleep on the rocky ground at Tower Lake in the Sierra. There are four horizontal bands of cream-colored rock wavering through the cliff face, and the dream said "those rock bands are your daughters.")

Where Dōgen and the Zen tradition would walk, chant a sutra, or do sitting meditation, the elder vernacular artisans of soul and spirit would play a flute, drum, dance, dream, listen for a song, go without food, and be available to communication with birds, animals, or rocks. There is a story of Coyote watching the yellow autumn cottonwood leaves float and eddy lightly down to the ground. It was so lovely to watch, he asked the cottonwood leaves if he might do it too. They warned him: "Coyote, you are too heavy and you have a body of bones and guts and muscle. We are light, we drift with the wind, but you would fall and be hurt." Coyote would hear none of it and insisted on climbing a cottonwood, edging far out onto a branch, and launching himself off. He fell and was killed. There's a caution here: do not be too hasty in setting out to "become one with." But, as we have heard, Coyote will roll over, reassemble his ribs, locate his paws, find a pebble with a dot of pitch on it to do for an eye, and trot off again.

Narratives are one sort of trace that we leave in the world. All our literatures are leavings—of the same order as the myths of wilderness peoples, who leave behind only stories and a few stone tools. Other orders of beings have their own literatures. Narrative in the deer world is a track of scents that is passed on from deer to deer with an art of interpretation which is instinctive. A literature of bloodstains, a bit of piss, a whiff of estrus, a hit of rut, a scrape on a sapling, and long gone. And there might be a "narrative theory" among these other beings—they might ruminate on "intersexuality" or "decomposition criticism."

I suspect that primary peoples all know that their myths are somehow "made up." They do not take them literally and at the same time they hold the stories very dear. Only upon being invaded by history and whipsawed by alien values do a people begin to declare that their myths are "literally true." This literalness in turn provokes skeptical questioning and the whole critical exercise. What a final refinement of confusion about the role of myths it is to declare that although they are not to be believed, they are nonetheless aesthetic and psychological constructs which bring order to an otherwise chaotic world and to which we should willfully commit ourselves! Dōgen's "You should know that even though all things are liberated and not tied to anything, they abide in their own phenomenal expression" is medicine for that. The "Mountains and Waters Sutra" is called a sutra not to assert that the "mountains and rivers of this moment" are a text, a system of symbols, a referential world of mirrors, but that this world in its actual existence is a complete presentation, an enactment—and that it stands for nothing.

Walking on Water

There's all sorts of walking—from heading out across the desert in a straight line to a sinuous weaving through undergrowth. Descending rocky ridges and talus slopes is a specialty in itself. It is an irregular dancing—always shifting—step of walk on slabs and scree. The breath and eye are always following this uneven rhythm. It is never paced or clocklike, but flexing—little jumps—sidesteps—going for the well-seen place to put a foot on a rock, hit flat, move on—zigzagging along and all deliberate. The alert eye looking ahead, picking the footholds to come, while never missing the step of the moment. The body-mind is so at one with this rough world that it makes these moves effortlessly once it has had a bit of practice. The mountain keeps up with the mountain.

In the year 1225 Dōgen was in his second year in South China. That year he walked out of the mountains and passed through the capital of the Southern Song dynasty, Hang-zhou, on his way north to the Wan-shou monastery at Mt. Jing. The only account of China left by Dōgen is notes on talks by the master Ru-jing (Kodera, 1980). I wonder what Dōgen would have said of city walking. Hang-zhou had level broad straight streets paralleling canals. He must have seen the many-storied houses, clean cobbled streets, theaters, markets, and innumerable restaurants. It had three thousand public baths. Marco Polo (who called it Quinsai) visited it twenty-five years later and estimated that it was probably the largest (at least a million people) and most affluent city in the world at that time (Gernet, 1962). Even today the people of Hang-zhou remember the lofty eleventh-century poet Su Shi, who built the causeway across West Lake when he was governor. At the time of Dōgen's walk North China was under the control of the Mongols, and Hang-zhou would fall to the Mongols in fifty-five more years.

The South China of that era sent landscape painting, calligraphy, both the Sōtō and Rinzai schools of Zen, and the vision of that great southern capital to Japan. The memory of Hang-zhou shaped both Osaka and Tokyo in their Tokugawa-era evolution. These two positions—one the austere Zen practice with its spare, clean halls, the other the possibility of a convivial urban life rich in festivals and theaters and restaurants—are two potent legacies of East Asia to the world. If Zen stands for the Far Eastern love of nature, Hang-zhou stands for the ideal of the city. Both are brimming with energy and life. Because most of the cities of the world are now mired in poverty, overpopulation, and pollution we have all the more reason to recover the dream. To neglect the city (in our hearts and minds for starters) is deadly, as James Hillman (1989, 169) says.

The "Mountains and Waters Sutra" goes on to say:

> All waters appear at the foot of the eastern mountains. Above all waters are all mountains. Walking beyond and walking within are both done on water. All mountains walk with their toes on all waters and splash there.

Dōgen finishes his meditation on mountains and waters with this: "When you investigate mountains thoroughly, this is the work of the mountains. Such mountains and waters of themselves become wise persons and, sages"—become sidewalk vendors and noodle-cooks, become marmots, ravens, graylings, carp, rattlesnakes, mosquitoes. *All* beings are "said" by the mountains and waters—even the clanking tread of a Caterpillar tractor, the gleam of the keys of a clarinet.

Ancient Forests
of the Far West

But ye shall destroy their altars,
    break their images, and cut down their groves.

EXODUS 34:13

After the Clearcut

We had a tiny dairy farm between Puget Sound and the north end of
Lake Washington, out in the cutover countryside. The bioregion-
alists call that part of northwestern Washington state "Ish" after
the suffix that means "river" in Salish. Rivers flowing into Puget
Sound are the Snohomish, Skykomish, Samamish, Duwamish, Stil-
laguamish.

    I remember my father dynamiting stumps and pulling the shards
out with a team. He cleared two acres and fenced it for three Guern-
seys. He built a two-story barn with stalls and storage for the cows
below and chickens above. He and my mother planted fruit trees,
kept geese, sold milk. Behind the back fence were the woods: a
second-growth jungle of alder and cascara trees with native black-
berry vines sprawling over the stumps. Some of the stumps were ten

feet high and eight or ten feet in diameter at the ground. High up the
sides were the notches the fallers had chopped in to support the steel-
tipped planks, the springboards, they stood on while felling. This
got them above the huge swell of girth at the bottom. Two or three
of the old trees had survived—small ones by comparison—and I
climbed those, especially one Western Red Cedar (*xelpai'its* in Snohomish) that I fancied became my advisor. Over the years I roamed
the second-growth Douglas Fir, Western Hemlock, and cedar forest
beyond the cow pasture, across the swamp, up a long slope, and into
a droughty stand of pines. The woods were more of a home than
home. I had a permanent campsite where I would sometimes cook
and spend the night.

When I was older I hiked into the old-growth stands of the foothill valleys of the Cascades and the Olympics where the shade-
tolerant skunk cabbage and devil's club underbrush is higher than
your head and the moss carpets are a foot thick. Here there is always
a deep aroma of crumbled wet organisms—fungus—and red rotten
logs and a few bushes of tart red thimbleberries. At the forest edges
are the thickets of salal with their bland seedy berries, the yellow salmonberries, and the tangles of vine-maples. Standing in the shade
you look out into the burns and the logged-off land and see the fire-
weed in bloom.

A bit older, I made it into the high mountains. The snowpeaks
were visible from near our place: in particular Mt. Baker and Glacier
Peak to the north and Mt. Rainier to the south. To the west, across
Puget Sound, the Olympics. Those unearthly glowing floating
snowy summits are a promise to the spirit. I first experienced one of
those distant peaks up close at fifteen, when I climbed Mt. Saint Hel-
ens. Rising at 3 A.M. at timberline and breaking camp so as to be on
glacier ice by six; standing in the rosy sunrise at nine thousand feet
on a frozen slope to the crisp tinkle of crampon points on ice—these
are some of the esoteric delights of mountaineering. To be immersed
in ice and rock and cold and upper space is to undergo an eery, rig-

orous initiation and transformation. Being above all the clouds with only a few other high mountains also in the sunshine, the human world still asleep under its gray dawn cloud blanket, is one of the first small steps toward Aldo Leopold's "think like a mountain." I made my way to most of the summits of the Northwest—Mt. Hood, Mt. Baker, Mt. Rainier, Mt. Adams, Mt. Stuart, and more —in subsequent years.

At the same time, I became more aware of the lowlands. Trucks ceaselessly rolled down the river valleys out of the Cascades loaded with great logs. Walking the low hills around our place near Lake City I realized that I had grown up in the aftermath of a clearcut, and that it had been only thirty-five or forty years since all those hills had been logged. I know now that the area had been home to some of the largest and finest trees the world has ever seen, an ancient forest of hemlock and Douglas Fir, a temperate-zone rainforest since before the glaciers. And I suspect that I was to some extent instructed by the ghosts of those ancient trees as they hovered near their stumps. I joined the Wilderness Society at seventeen, subscribed to *Living Wilderness*, and wrote letters to Congress about forestry issues in the Olympics.

But I was also instructed by the kind of work done by my uncles, our neighbors, the workers of the whole Pacific Northwest. My father put me on one end of a two-man crosscut saw when I was ten and gave me the classic instruction of "don't ride the saw"—don't push, only pull—and I loved the clean swish and ring of the blade, the rhythm, the comradeship, the white curl of the wood that came out with the rakers, the ritual of setting the handles, and the sprinkle of kerosene (to dissolve pitch) on the blade and into the kerf. We cut rounds out of down logs to split for firewood. (Unemployed men during the Depression felled the tall cedar stumps left from the first round of logging to buck them into blanks and split them with froes for the hand-split cedar shake trade.) We felled trees to clear pasture. We burned huge brush-piles.

People love to do hard work together and to feel that the work is real; that is to say primary, productive, needed. Knowing and enjoying the skills of our hands and our well-made tools is fundamental. It is a tragic dilemma that much of the best work men do together is no longer quite right. The fine information on the techniques of hand-whaling and all the steps of the flensing and rendering described in *Moby Dick* must now, we know, be measured against the terrible specter of the extinction of whales. Even the farmer or the carpenter is uneasy: pesticides, herbicides, creepy subsidies, welfare water, cheap materials, ugly subdivisions, walls that won't last. Who can be proud? And our conservationist-environmentalist-moral outrage is often (in its frustration) aimed at the logger or the rancher, when the real power is in the hands of people who make unimaginably larger sums of money, people impeccably groomed, excellently educated at the best universities— male and female alike—eating fine foods and reading classy literature, while orchestrating the investment and legislation that ruin the world. As I grew into young manhood in the Pacific Northwest, advised by a cedar tree, learning the history of my region, practicing mountaineering, studying the native cultures, and inventing the little rituals that kept my spirit sane, I was often supporting myself by the woodcutting skills I learned on the Depression stump-farm.

At Work in the Woods

In 1952 and '53 I worked for the Forest Service as a lookout in the northern Cascades. The following summer, wanting to see new mountains, I applied to a national forest in the Mt. Rainier area. I had already made my way to the Packwood Ranger Station and purchased my summer's supply of lookout groceries when the word came to the district (from Washington, D.C.) that I should be fired.

That was the McCarthy era and the Velde Committee hearings were taking place in Portland. Many of my acquaintances were being named on TV. It was the end of my career as a seasonal forestry worker for the government.

I was totally broke, so I decided to go back to the logging industry. I hitched east of the Oregon Cascades to the Warm Springs Indian Reservation and checked in with the Warm Springs Lumber Company. I had scaled timber here the summer of '51, and now they hired me on as a chokersetter. This is the lava plateau country south of the Columbia River and in the drainage of the Deschutes, up to the headwaters of the Warm Springs River. We were cutting old-growth Ponderosa Pine on the middle slopes of the east side, a fragrant open forest of massive straight-trunked trees growing on volcanic soils. The upper edge verged into the alpine life-zone, and the lower edge—farther and farther out into the desert—became sagebrush by degrees. The logging was under contract with the tribal council. The proceeds were to benefit the people as a whole.

11 August '54
Chokersetting today. Madras in the evening for beer. Under the shadow of Mt. Jefferson. Long cinnamon-colored logs. This is "pine" and it belongs to "Indians"—what a curious knotting-up. That these Indians & these trees, that coexisted for centuries, should suddenly be possessor and possessed. Our *concepts to be sure.*

I had no great problem with that job. Unlike the thick-growing Douglas Fir rainforests west of the Cascades, where there are arguments for clearcutting, the drier pine forests are perfect for selective cutting. Here the slopes were gentle and they were taking no more than 40 percent of the canopy. A number of healthy mid-sized seed trees were left standing. The D8 Cats could weave their way through without barking the standing trees.

Chokersetting is part of the skidding operation. First into the woods are the timber cruisers who estimate the standing board feet and mark the trees. Then come the road-building Cats and graders. Right on their heels are the gypo fallers—gypos get paid for quantity produced rather than a set wage—and then comes the skidding crew. West-of-the-mountains skidding is typically a high-lead or skyline cable operation where the logs are yarded in via a cable system strung out of a tall spar tree. In the east-side pine forest the skidding is done with top-size Caterpillar tractors. The Cat pulls a crawler-tread "arch" trailer behind it with a cable running from the Cat's aft winch up and over the pulley-wheel at the top of the arch, and then down where the cable divides into three massive chains that end in heavy steel hooks, the butt-hooks. I was on a team of two that worked behind one Cat. It was a two-Cat show.

Each Cat drags the felled and bucked logs to the landing—where they are loaded on trucks—from its own set of skid trails. While it is dragging a load of logs in, the chokersetters (who stay behind up the skid trails) are studying the next haul. You pick out the logs you'll give the Cat next trip, and determine the sequence in which you'll hook them so they will not cross each other, flip, twist over, snap live trees down, hang up on stumps, or make other dangerous and complicating moves. Chokersetters should be light and wiry. I wore White's caulked logger boots with steel points like tiny weasel-fangs set in the sole. I was thus enabled to run out and along a huge log or up its slope with perfect footing, while looking at the lay and guessing the physics of its mass in motion. The Cat would be coming back up the skid trail dragging the empty choker cables and would swing in where I signaled. I'd pluck two or three chokers off the butt-hooks and drag the sixteen-foot cables behind me into the logs and brush. The Cat would go on out to the other chokersetter who would take off his cables and do the same.

As the Cat swung out and was making its turnaround, the chokersetters would be down in dirt and duff, ramming the knobbed end of the choker under the log, bringing it up and around, and hooking it into the sliding steel catch called a "bell" that would noose up on the log when the choker pulled taut. The Cat would back its arch into where I stood, holding up chokers. I'd hook the first "D"—the ring on the free end of the choker—over the butt-hook and send the Cat to the next log. It could swing ahead and pull alongside while I leaped atop another load and hung the next choker onto the butt-hook. Then the winch on the rear of the Cat would wind in, and the butts of the logs would be lifted clear of the ground, hanging them up in the arch between the two crawler-tread wheels.

> Stood straight
> > holding the choker high
> As the Cat swung back the arch
> > piss-firs falling,
> Limbs snapping on the tin hat
> > bright D caught on
> Swinging butt-hooks
> > ringing against cold steel.
> > > (from *Myths and Texts*)

The next question was, how would they fan out? My Cat-skinner was Little Joe, nineteen and just recently married, chewing plug and always joking. I'd give him the highball sign and at the same time run back out the logs, even as he started pulling, to leap off the back end. Never stand between a fan of lying logs, they say. When the tractor hauls out they might swing in and snap together—"Chokersetters lose their legs that way." And don't stand anywhere near a snag when the load goes out. If the load even lightly brushes it, the top of the snag, or the whole thing, might come down. I saw a dead schoolmarm (a tree with a crotch in its top third) snap off and fall like that, grazing the tin hat of a chokersetter called Stubby. He was lucky.

The D8 tears through piss-fir
Scrapes the seed-pine
                        chipmunks flee,
A black ant carries an egg
Aimlessly from the battered ground.
Yellowjackets swarm and circle
Above the crushed dead log, their home.
Pitch oozes from barked
                        trees still standing,
Mashed bushes make strange smells.
Lodgepole pines are brittle.
Camprobbers flutter to watch.

I learned tricks, placements, pulls from the experienced chokerset-ters—ways to make a choker cable swing a log over, even to make it jump out from under. Ways and sequences of hooking on chokers that when first in place looked like a messy spiderweb, but when the Cat pulled out, the tangle of logs would right itself and the cables mysteriously fan out into a perfect pull with nothing crossed. We were getting an occasional eight-foot-diameter tree and many five and six footers: these were some of the most perfect Ponderosa Pine I have ever seen. We also had White Fir, Douglas Fir, and some larch.

I was soon used to the grinding squeaking roar and rattle of the Cat, the dust, and the rich smells that rose from the bruised and stirred-up soil and plant life. At lunchtime, when the machinery was silent, we'd see deer picking their way through the torn-up woods. A Black Bear kept breaking into the crummy truck to get at the lunches until someone shot him and the whole camp ate him for dinner. There was no rancor about the bear, and no sense of conquest about the logging work. The men were stoic, skillful, a bit over-worked, and full of terrible (but funny!) jokes and expressions. Many of them were living on the Rez, which was shared by Wasco, Wishram, and Shoshone people. The lumber company gave priority to the Native American locals in hiring.

Ray Wells, a big Nisqually, and I
    each set a choker
On the butt-logs of two big Larch
In a thornapple thicket and a swamp.
     waiting for the Cat to come back,
"Yesterday we gelded some ponies
"My father-in-law cut the skin on the balls
"He's a Wasco and don't speak English
"He grabs a handful of tubes and somehow
     cuts the right ones.
"The ball jumps out, the horse screams
"But he's all tied up.
The Caterpillar clanked back down.
In the shadow of that racket
     diesel and iron tread
I thought of Ray Wells' tipi out on the sage flat
The gelded ponies
Healing and grazing in the dead white heat.

There were also old white guys who had worked in the lumber industry all their lives: one had been active in the Industrial Workers
of the World, the "Wobblies," and had no use for the later unions. I
told him about my grandfather, who had soapboxed for the Wobblies in Seattle's Yesler Square, and my Uncle Roy, whose wife Anna
was also the chief cook at a huge logging camp at Gray's Harbor
around World War I. I told him of the revived interest in anarcho-
syndicalism among some circles in Portland. He said he hadn't had
anyone talk Wobbly talk with him in twenty years, and he relished
it. His job, knotbumper, kept him at the landing where the skidding Cats dropped the logs off. Although the buckers cut the limbs
off, sometimes they left stubs which would make the logs hard to
load and stack. He chopped off stubs with a double-bitted axe. Ed
had a circular wear-mark impressed in the rear pocket of his stagged

jeans: it was from his round axe-sharpening stone. Between loads he constantly sharpened his axe, and he could shave a paper-thin slice off a Day's Work plug, his chew, with the blade.

> Ed McCullough, a logger for thirty-five years
> Reduced by the advent of chainsaws
> To chopping off knots at the landing:
> "I don't have to take this kind of shit,
> Another twenty years
>   and I'll tell 'em to shove it"
>   (he was sixty-five then)
> In 1934 they lived in shanties
> At Hooverville, Sullivan's Gulch.
> When the Portland-bound train came through
> The trainmen tossed off coal.

> "Thousands of boys shot and beat up
> For wanting a good bed, good pay,
>   decent food, in the woods—"
> No one knew what it meant:
> "Soldiers of Discontent."

On one occasion a Cat went to the landing pulling only one log, and not the usual 32-foot length but a 16. Even though it was only half-length the Cat could barely drag it. We had to rig two chokers to get around it, and there was not much pigtail left. I know now that the tree had been close to being of record size. The largest Ponderosa Pine in the world, near Mt. Adams, which I went out some miles of dust dirt roads to see, isn't much larger around than was that tree.

How could one not regret seeing such a massive tree go out for lumber? It was an elder, a being of great presence, a witness to the centuries. I saved a few of the tan free-form scales from the bark of that log and placed them on the tiny altar I kept on a box by my bunk at the logging camp. It and the other offerings (a flicker feather, a bit of broken bird's-egg, some obsidian, and a postcard picture of the Bodhisattva of Transcendent Intelligence, Manjusri) were not "my" offerings to the forest, but the forest's offerings to all of us. I guess I was just keeping some small note of it.

All of the trees in the Warm Springs forest were old growth. They were perfect for timber, too, most of them rot-free. I don't doubt that the many seed-trees and smaller trees left standing have flourished, and that the forest came back in good shape. A forester working for the Bureau of Indian Affairs and the tribal council had planned that cut.

Or did it come back in good shape? I don't know if the Warm Springs timber stands have already been logged again. They should not have been, but—

There was a comforting conservationist rhetoric in the world of forestry and lumber from the mid-thirties to the late fifties. The heavy clearcutting that has now devastated the whole Pacific slope from the Kern River to Sitka, Alaska, had not yet begun. In those days forestry professionals still believed in selective logging and actually practiced sustained yield. Those were, in hindsight, the last years of righteous forest management in the United States.

Evergreen

The raw dry country of the American West had an odd effect on American politics. It transformed and even radicalized some people. Once the West was closed to homesteading and the unclaimed lands became public domain, a few individuals realized that the future of these lands was open to public discussion. Some went from exploration and appreciation of wilderness to political activism.

Daoist philosophers tell us that surprise and subtle instruction might come forth from the Useless. So it was with the wastelands of the American West—inaccessible, inhospitable, arid, and forbidding to the eyes of most early Euro-Americans. The Useless Lands became the dreaming place of a few nineteenth- and early-twentieth-century men and women (John Wesley Powell on matters of water and public lands, Mary Austin on Native Americans, deserts, women) who went out into the space and loneliness and returned from their quests not only to criticize the policies and assumptions of the expanding United States but, in the name of wilderness and the commons, to hoist the sails that are filling with wind today. Some of the newly established public lands did have potential uses for lumber, grazing, and mining. But in the case of timber and grass, the best lands were already in private hands. What went into the public domain (or occasionally into Indian reservation status) was—by the standards of those days—marginal land. The off-limits bombing ranges and nuclear test sites of the Great Basin are public domain lands, too, borrowed by the military from the BLM.

So the forests that were set aside for the initial Forest Reserves were not at that time considered prime timber land. Early-day lumber interests in the Pacific Northwest went for the dense, low-elevation conifer forests like those around the house I grew up in or those forests right on saltwater or near rivers. This accessible land, once clearcut, became real estate, but the farther reaches were kept by the big companies as commercial forest. Much of the Olympic Peninsula forest land is privately held. Only by luck and chance did an occasional low-elevation stand such as the Hoh River forest in Olympic National Park, or Jedediah Smith redwoods in California, end up in public domain. It is by virtue of these islands of forest survivors that we can still see what the primeval forest of the West Coast—in its densest and most concentrated incarnation—was like. "Virgin forest" it was once called, a telling term. Then it was called "old growth" or in certain cases "climax." Now we begin to call it "ancient forest."

On the rainy Pacific slope there were million-acre stands that had been coevolving for millennia, possibly for over a million years. Such forests are the fullest examples of ecological process, containing as they do huge quantities of dead and decaying matter as well as the new green and preserving the energy pathways of both detritus and growth. An ancient forest will have many truly large old trees—some having craggy, broken-topped, mossy "dirty" crowns with much organic accumulation, most with holes and rot in them. There will be standing snags and tons of dead down logs. These character-istics, although not delightful to lumbermen ("overripe"), are what make an ancient forest more than a stand of timber: it is a palace of organisms, a heaven for many beings, a temple where life deeply in-vestigates the puzzle of itself. Living activity goes right down to and under the "ground"—the litter, the duff. There are termites, larvae, millipedes, mites, earthworms, springtails, pillbugs, and the fine threads of fungus woven through. "There are as many as 5,500 in-dividuals (not counting the earthworms and nematodes) per square foot of soil to a depth of 13 inches. As many as 70 different species have been collected from less than a square foot of rich forest soil. The total animal population of the soil and litter together probably approaches 10,000 animals per square foot" (Robinson, 1988, 87).

The dominant conifers in this forest, Douglas Fir, Western Red Cedar, Western Hemlock, Noble Fir, Sitka Spruce, and Coastal Redwood, are all long-lived and grow to great size. They are often the longest-lived of their genera. The old forests of the western slopes support some of the highest per-acre biomass—total living matter—the world has seen, approached only by some of the Aus-tralian eucalyptus forests. An old-growth temperate hardwood for-est, and also the tropical forests, average around 153 tons per acre. The west slope forests of the Oregon Cascades averaged 433 tons per acre. At the very top of the scale, the coastal redwood forests have been as high as 1,831 tons per acre (Waring and Franklin, 1979).

Forest ecologists and paleoecologists speculate on how such a massive forest came into existence. It seems the western forest of twenty or so million years ago was largely deciduous hardwoods—ash, maple, beech, oak, chestnut, elm, gingko—with conifers only at the highest elevations. Twelve to eighteen million years ago, the conifers began to occupy larger areas and then made continuous connection with each other along the uplands. By a million and a half years ago, in the early Pleistocene, the conifers had completely taken over and the forest was essentially as it is now. Forests of the type that had prevailed earlier, the hardwoods, survive today in the eastern United States and were also the original vegetation (before agriculture and early logging) of China and Japan. Visiting Great Smoky Mountains National Park today might give you an idea of what the mountain forests outside the old Chinese capital of Xian, known earlier as Ch'ang-an, looked like in the ninth century.

In the other temperate-zone forests of the world, conifers are a secondary and occasional presence. The success of the West Coast conifers can be attributed, it seems, to a combination of conditions: relatively cool and quite dry summers (which do not serve deciduous trees so well) combined with mild wet winters (during which the conifers continue to photosynthesize) and an almost total absence of typhoons. The enormous size of the trunks helps to store moisture and nutrients against drought years. The forests are steady-growing and productive (from a timber standpoint) while young, and these particular species keep growing and accumulating biomass long after most other temperate-zone trees have reached equilibrium.

Here we find the northern Flying Squirrel (which lives on truffles) and its sacred enemy the Spotted Owl. The Douglas Squirrel (or Chickaree) lives here, as does its sacred enemy the treetop-dashing Pine Marten that can run a squirrel down. Black Bear seeks the grubs in long-dead logs in her steady ambling search. These and hosts of others occupy the deep shady stable halls—less wind, less swing of temperature, steady moisture—of the huge tree groves. There are treetop-dwelling Red-backed Voles who have been two hundred feet high in the canopy for hundreds of generations, some of whom have never descended to the ground (Maser, 1989). In a way the web that holds it all together is the mycelia, the fungus-threads that mediate between root-tips of plants and chemistry of soils, bringing nutrients in. This association is as old as plants with roots. The whole of the forest is supported by this buried network.

The forests of the maritime Pacific Northwest are the last remaining forests of any size left in the temperate zone. Plato's *Critias* passage (¶111) says: "In the primitive state of the country [Attica] its mountains were high hills covered with soil . . . and there was abundance of wood in the mountains. Of this last the traces still remain, for although some of the mountains now only afford sustenance to bees, not so very long ago there were still to be seen roofs of timber cut from trees growing there . . . and there were many other high trees. . . . Moreover the land reaped the benefit of the annual rainfall, not as now losing the water which flows off the bare earth into the sea." The cautionary history of the Mediterranean forests is well known. Much of this destruction has taken place in recent centuries, but it was already well under way, especially in the lowlands, during the classical period. In neolithic times the whole basin had perhaps 500 million acres of forest. The higher-elevation forests are all that survive, and even they occupy only 30 percent of the mountain zone—about 45 million acres. Some 100 million acres of land once densely covered with pine, oak, ash, laurel, and myrtle now have only traces of vegetation. There is a more sophisticated vocabulary in the Mediterranean for postforest or nonforest plant communities than we have in California (where everything scrubby is called chaparral). *Maquis* is the term for oak, olive, myrtle, and juniper scrub. An assembly of low waxy drought-resistant shrubs is called *garrigue*. *Batha* is open bare rock and eroding ground with scattered low shrubs and annuals.

People who live there today do not even know that their gray rocky hills were once rich in groves and wildlife. The intensified destruction was a function of the *type* of agriculture. The small self-sufficient peasant farms and their commons began to be replaced by the huge slave-run *latifundia* estates owned in absentia and planned according to central markets. What wildlife was left in the commons might then be hunted out by the new owners, the forest sold for cash, and field crops extended for what they were worth. "The cities of the Mediterranean littoral became deeply involved in an intensive region-wide trade, with cheap manufactured products, intensified markets and factory-like industrial production. . . . These developments in planned colonization, economic planning, world currencies and media for exchange had drastic consequences for the natural vegetation from Spain through to India" (Thirgood, 1981, 29).

China's lowland hardwood forests gradually disappeared as agriculture spread and were mostly gone by about thirty-five hundred years ago. (The Chinese philosopher Meng-zi commented on the risks of clearcutting in the fourth century B.C.) The composition of the Japanese forest has been altered by centuries of continuous logging. The Japanese sawmills are now geared down to about eight-inch logs. The original deciduous hardwoods are found only in the most remote mountains. The prized aromatic Hinoki (the Japanese chamaecypress), which is essential to shrine and temple buildings, is now so rare that logs large enough for renovating traditional structures must be imported from the West Coast. Here it is known as Port Orford Cedar, found only in southern Oregon and in the Siskiyou Mountains of northern California. It was used for years to make arrow-shafts. Now Americans cannot afford it. No other softwood on earth commands such prices as the Japanese buyers are willing to pay for this species.

Commercial West Coast logging started around the 1870s. For decades it was all below the four-thousand-foot level. That was the era of the two-man saw, the double-bitted axe-cut undercuts, springboards, the kerosene bottle with a hook wired onto it stuck in the bark. Gypo handloggers felled into the saltwater bays of Puget Sound and rafted their logs to the mills. Then came steam donkey-engine yarders and ox teams, dragging the huge logs down corduroy skidroads or using immense wooden logging wheels that held the butt end aloft as the tail of the log dragged. The ox teams were re-placed by narrow-gauge trains, and the steam donkeys by diesel. The lower elevations of the West Coast were effectively totally clear-cut.

Chris Maser (1989, xviii) says: "Every increase in the technology of logging and the utilization of wood fiber has expedited the ex-ploitation of forests; thus from 1935 through 1980 the annual vol-ume of timber cut has increased geometrically by 4.7% per year. . . . By the 1970s, 65% of the timber cut occurred above 4,000 feet in elevation, and because the average tree harvested has become pro-gressively younger and smaller, the increase in annual acreage cut has been five times greater than the increase in volume cut during the last 40 years."

During these years the trains were replaced by trucks, and the high-lead yarders in many cases were replaced by the more mobile crawler-tread tractors we call Cats. From the late forties on, the graceful, musical Royal Chinook two-man falling saws were hung up on the walls of the barns, and the gasoline chainsaw became the faller's tool of choice. By the end of World War II the big logging companies had (with a few notable exceptions) managed to overex-ploit and mismanage their own timberlands and so they now turned to the federal lands, the people's forests, hoping for a bailout. So much for the virtues of private forest landowners—their history is abysmal—but there are still ill-informed privatization romantics who argue that the public lands should be sold to the highest bid-ders.

San Francisco 2 × 4s
    were the woods around Seattle:

Someone killed and someone built, a house,
 a forest, wrecked or raised
All America hung on a hook
 & burned by men in their own praise.

Before World War II the U.S. Forest Service played the role of a true conservation agency and spoke against the earlier era of clearcutting. It usually required its contractors to do selective logging to high standards. The allowable cut was much smaller. It went from 3.5 billion board feet in 1950 to 13.5 billion feet in 1970. After 1961 the new Forest Service leadership cosied up to the industry, and the older conservation-oriented personnel were washed out in waves through the sixties and seventies. The USFS now hires mostly road-building engineers. Their silviculturists think of themselves as fiber-growing engineers, and some profess to see no difference between a monoculture plantation of even-age seedlings and a wild forest (or so said Tahoe National Forest silviculturist Phil Aune at a public hearing on the management plan in 1986). The public relations people still cycle the conservation rhetoric of the thirties, as though the Forest Service had never permitted a questionable clearcut or sold old-growth timber at a financial loss.

The legislative mandate of the Forest Service leaves no doubt about its responsibility to manage the forest lands *as forests*, which means that lumber is only one of the values to be considered. It is clear that the forests must be managed in a way that makes them permanently sustainable. But Congress, the Department of Agriculture, and business combine to find ways around these restraints. *Renewable* is confused with *sustainable* (just because certain organisms keep renewing themselves does not mean they will do so—especially if abused—forever), and *forever*—the length of time a forest should continue to flourish—is changed to mean "about a hundred and fifty years." Despite the overwhelming evidence of mismanagement that environmental groups have brought against the Forest Service bureaucracy, it arrogantly and stubbornly resists what has become a clear public call for change. So much for the icon of "management" with its uncritical acceptance of the economic speed-trip of modern times (generating faster and faster logging rotations in the woods) as against: slow cycles.

We ask for slower rotations, genuine streamside protection, fewer roads, no cuts on steep slopes, only occasional shelterwood cuts, and only the most prudent application of the appropriate smaller clear-cut. We call for a return to selective logging, and to all-age trees, and to serious heart and mind for the protection of endangered species. (The Spotted Owl, the Fisher, and the Pine Marten are only part of the picture.) There should be *absolutely no more logging* in the remaining ancient forests. In addition we need the establishment of habitat corridors to keep the old-growth stands from becoming impoverished biological islands.

Many of the people in the U.S. Forest Service would agree that such practices are essential to genuine sustainability. They are constrained by the tight net of exploitative policies forced on them by Congress and industry. With good practices North America could maintain a lumber industry and protect a halfway decent amount of wild forest for ten thousand years. That is about the same number of years as the age of the continuously settled village culture of the Wei River valley in China, a span of time which is not excessive for humans to consider and plan by. As it is, the United States is suffering a net loss of 900,000 acres of forest per year (*Newsweek*, 2 October 1989). Of that loss, an estimated 60,000 acres is ancient forest (Wilson, 1989, 112).

The deep woods turn, turn, and turn again. The ancient forests of the West are still around us. All the houses of San Francisco, Eureka, Corvallis, Portland, Seattle, Longview, are built with those old bodies: the 2×4s and siding are from the logging of the 1910s and 1920s. Strip the paint in an old San Francisco apartment and you find prime-quality coastal redwood panels. We live out our daily lives in the shelter of ancient trees. Our great-grandchildren will more likely have to live in the shelter of riverbed-aggregate. Then the forests of the past will be truly entirely gone.

Out in the forest it takes about the same number of years as the tree lived for a fallen tree to totally return to the soil. If societies could learn to live by such a pace there would be no shortages, no extinctions. There would be clear streams, and the salmon would always return to spawn.

> A virgin
> Forest
> Is ancient; many-
> Breasted,
> Stable; at
> Climax.

Excursus: Sailor Meadow, Sierra Nevada

We were walking in mid-October down to Sailor Meadow (about 5,800 feet), to see an old stand on a broad bench above the north fork of the American River in the northern Sierra Nevada. At first we descended a ridge-crest through chinquapin and manzanita, looking north to the wide dome of Snow Mountain and the cliffs above Royal Gorge. The faint trail leveled out and we left it to go to the stony hills at the north edge of the hanging basin. Sitting beneath a cedar growing at the top of the rocks we ate lunch.

Then we headed southwest over rolls of forested stony formations and eventually more gentle slopes into a world of greater and greater trees. For hours we were in the company of elders.

Sugar Pines predominate. There are properly mature symmetrical trees a hundred and fifty feet high that hold themselves upright and keep their branches neatly arranged. But then *beyond* them, *above* them, loom the *ancient trees*: huge, loopy, trashy, and irregular. Their bark is redder and the plates more spread, they have fewer branches, and those surviving branches are great in girth and curve wildly. Each one is unique and goofy. Mature Incense Cedar. Some large Red Fir. An odd Douglas Fir. A few great Jeffrey Pine. (Some of the cedars have catface burn marks from some far-back fire at their bases—all on the northwest side. None of the other trees show these burn marks.)

And many snags, in all conditions: some just recently expired with red or brown dead needles still clinging, some deader yet with plates of bark hanging from the trunk (where bats nest), some pure white smooth dead ones with hardly any limbs left, but with an occasional neat woodpecker hole; and finally the ancient dead: all soft and rotten while yet standing.

Many have fallen. There are freshly fallen snags (which often take a few trees with them) and the older fallen snags. Firm down logs you must climb over, or sometimes you can walk their length, and logs that crumble as you climb them. Logs of still another age have gotten soft and begun to fade, leaving just the pitchy heartwood core and some pitchy rot-proof limbs as signs. And then there are some long subtle hummocks that are the last trace of an old gone log. The straight line of mushrooms sprouting along a smooth ground surface is the final sign, the last ghost, of a tree that "died" centuries ago.

A carpet of young trees coming in—from six inches tall to twenty feet, all sizes—waiting down here on the forest floor for the big snags standing up there dead to keel over and make more canopy space. Sunny, breezy, warm, open, light—but the great trees are all around us. Their trunks fill the sky and reflect a warm golden light. The whole canopy has that sinewy look of ancient trees. Their needles are distinctive tiny patterns against the sky—the Red Fir most strict and fine.

The forests of the Sierra Nevada, like those farther up the West Coast, date from that time when the earlier deciduous hardwood forests were beginning to fade away before the spreading success of the conifers. It is a million years of "family" here, too, the particular composition of local forest falling and rising in elevation with the ice age temperature fluctuations, advancing or retreating from north and south slope positions, but keeping the several plant communities together even as the boundaries of their zones flowed uphill or down through the centuries. Absorbing fire, adapting to the summer drought, flowing through the beetle-kill years; always a web reweaving. Acorns feeding deer, manzanita feeding robins and raccoons, Madrone feeding Band-tailed Pigeon, porcupine gnawing young cedar bark, bucks thrashing their antlers in the willows.

The middle-elevation Sierra forest is composed of Sugar Pine, Ponderosa Pine, Incense Cedar, Douglas Fir, and at slightly higher elevations Jeffrey Pine, White Fir, and Red Fir. All of these trees are long-lived. The Sugar Pine and Ponderosa are the largest of all pines. Black Oak, Live Oak, Tanbark Oak, and Madrone are the common hardwoods.

The Sierra forest is sunny-shady and dry for fully half the year. The loose litter, the crackliness, the dustiness of the duff, the curl of crisp Madrone leaves on the ground, the little coins of fallen manzanita leaves. The pine-needle floor is crunchy, the air is slightly resinous and aromatic, there is a delicate brushing of spiderwebs everywhere. Summer forest: intense play of sun and the vegetation in still steady presence—not giving up water, not wilting, not stressing, just quietly holding. Shrubs with small, aromatic, waxy, tough leaves. The shrub color is often blue-gray.

The forest was fire-adapted over the millennia and is extremely resistant to wildfire once the larger underbrush has burnt or died away. The early emigrants described driving their wagons through parklike forests of great trees as they descended the west slope of the range. The early logging was followed by devastating fires. Then came the suppression of fires by the forest agencies, and that led to the brushy understory that is so common to the Sierra now. The Sailor Meadow forest is a spacious, open, fireproof forest from the past.

At the south end of the small meadow the area is named for, beyond a thicket of aspen, standing within a grove of flourishing fir, is a remarkably advanced snag. It once was a pine over two hundred feet tall. Now around the base all the sapwood has peeled away, and what's holding the bulky trunk up is a thin column of heartwood which is itself all punky, shedding, and frazzled. The great rotten thing has a lean as well! Any moment it might go.

How curious it would be to die and then remain standing for another century or two. To enjoy "dead verticality." If humans could do it we would hear news like, "Henry David Thoreau finally toppled over." The human community, when healthy, is like an ancient forest. The little ones are in the shade and shelter of the big ones, even rooted in their lost old bodies. All ages, and all together growing and dying. What some silviculturists call for—"even-age management," plantations of trees the same size growing up together— seems like rationalistic utopian totalitarianism. We wouldn't think of letting our children live in regimented institutions with no parental visits and all their thinking shaped by a corps of professionals who just follow official manuals (written by people who never raised kids). Why should we do it to our forests?

"All-age unmanaged"—that's a natural community, human or other. The industry prizes the younger and middle-aged trees that keep their symmetry, keep their branches even of length and angle. But let there also be really old trees who can give up all sense of propriety and begin throwing their limbs out in extravagant gestures, dancelike poses, displaying their insouciance in the face of mortality, holding themselves available to whatever the world and the weather might propose. I look up to them: they are like the Chinese Immortals, they are Han-shan and Shi-de sorts of characters—to have lived that long is to have permission to be eccentric, to be the poets and painters among trees, laughing, ragged, and fearless. They make me almost look forward to old age.

In the fir grove we can smell mushrooms, and then we spot them along the base of rotten logs. A cluster of Elegant Polypores, a Cortinarius, and in the open, pushing up dry needles from below, lots of russula and boletus. Some scooped-out hollows where the deer have dug them out. Deer love mushrooms.

We tried to go straight across the southern end of the meadow but it was squishy wet beneath the dry-looking collapsed dead plants and grasses, so we went all the way around the south end through more aspen and found (and saved) more mushrooms. Clouds started blowing in from the south and the breeze filled the sky with dry pine needles raining down. It was late afternoon, so we angled up steep slopes cross-country following deer-paths for an hour and found the overgrown trail to an abandoned mine, and it led us back to the truck.

Us Yokels

This little account of the great forests of the West Coast can be taken as a model of what has been happening elsewhere on the planet. All the natural communities of the world have been, in their own way, "ancient" and every natural community, like a family, includes the infants, the adolescents, the mature adults, the elders. From the corner of the forest that has had a recent burn, with its fire-weed and blackberries, to the elder moist dark groves—this is the range of the integrity of the whole. The old stands of hoary trees (or half-rotten saguaro in the Sonoran Desert or thick-boled well-established old manzanita in the Sierra foothills) are the grandparents and information-holders of their communities. A community needs its elders to continue. Just as you could not grow culture out of a population of kindergarten children, a forest cannot realize its own natural potential without the seed-reservoirs, root-fungus threads, birdcalls, and magical deposits of tiny feces that are the gift from the old to the young. Chris Maser says, "We need ancient forests for the survival of ancient forests."

When the moldboard plows of the early midwestern farmers "cut the grass roots—a sound that reminded one of a zipper being opened or closed—a new way of life opened, which simultaneously closed, probably forever, a long line of ecosystems stretching back thirty million years" (Jackson, 1987, 78). But the oldest continuous ecosystems on earth are the moist tropical forests, which in Southeast Asia are estimated to date back one hundred million years.

> Thin arching buttressing boles of the white-barked tall
> straight trees, Staghorn ferns leaning out from the limbs
> and the crotches up high. Trees they call brushbox,
> coachwood, crabapple, Australian red cedar (names
> brought from Europe)—and Red carrabeen, Yellow
> carrabeen, Stinging-trees, Deep blue openings leaning
> onward.
>
> Light of green arch of leaves far above
> Drinking the water that flows through the roots
> Of the forest, Terania creek, flowing out of Pangaia,
> Down from Gondwanaland,
> Stony soil, sky bottom shade
>
> Long ago stone deep
> Roots from the sky
> Clear water down through the roots
> Of the trees that reach high in the shade
> Birdcalls bring us awake
> Whiplash birdcalls laugh us awake—
>
> Booyong, Carrabeen, Brushbox, Black butt, Wait-a-
>   while
> (Eucalypts dry land thin soil succeeders
> Searching scrabbly ground for seventy million years—)
>
> But these older tribes of trees
> Travel always as a group.

Looking out from the cliffs
On the ridge above treetops,
Sitting up in the dust ledge shelter
Where we lived all those lives.

Queensland, 1981

A multitude of corporations are involved in the deforestation of the tropics. Some got their start logging in Michigan or the Pacific Northwest—Georgia Pacific and Scott Paper are now in the Philippines, Southeast Asia, or Latin America with the same bright-colored crawler tractors and the buzzing yellow chainsaws. In the summer of 1987 in Brazil's western territory of Rondonia—as part of the chaotic "conversion" of Amazonia to other uses—an area of forest the size of Oregon was in flames. One sometimes hears the innocent opinion that everyone is a city-dweller now. That time may be coming, but at the moment the largest single population in the world is people of several shades of color farming in the warmer zones. Up until recently a large part of that realm was in trees, and the deep-forest-dwelling cultures had diverse and successful ways to live there. In those times of smaller population, the long-rotation slash-and-burn style of farming mixed with foraging posed no ecological threat. Today a combination of large-scale logging, agribusiness development, and massive dam projects threatens every corner of the backcountry.

In Brazil there is a complex set of adversaries. On one side the national government with its plans for development is allied with multinationals, wealthy cattle interests, and impoverished mainstream peasants. On the other side, resisting deforestation, are the public and private foresters and scientists making cause with the small local lumber firms, the established jungle-edge peasants, environmental organizations, and the forest-dwelling tribes. The Third World governments usually deny "native title" and the validity of communal forest ownership histories, such as the *adat* system of the

Penan of Sarawak, a sophisticated multidimensional type of commons. The Penan people must put their bodies in the road to protest logging trucks *in their own homeland* and then go to jail as criminals.

Third World policies in regard to wilderness all too often run a direction set by India in 1938 when it opened the tribal forest lands of Assam to outside settlement saying "indigenous people alone would be unable, without the aid of immigrant settlers, to develop the province's enormous wasteland resources within a reasonable period" (Richards and Tucker, 1988, 107). All too many people in power in the governments and universities of the world seem to carry a prejudice against the natural world—and also against the past, against history. It seems Americans would live by a Chamber-of-Commerce Creationism that declares itself satisfied with a divinely presented Shopping Mall. The integrity and character of our own ancestors is dismissed with "I couldn't live like that" by people who barely know how to live *at all*. An ancient forest is seen as a kind of overripe garbage, not unlike the embarrassing elderly.

> Forestry. "How
> Many people
> Were harvested
> In Viet-nam?"
>
> Clear-cut. "Some
> Were children,
> Some were over-ripe."

The societies that live by the old ways (Snyder, 1977) had some remarkable skills. For those who live by foraging—the original forest botanists and zoologists—the jungle is a rich supply of fibers, poisons, medicines, intoxicants, detoxicants, containers, waterproofing, food, dyes, glues, incense, amusement, companionship, inspiration, and also stings, blows, and bites. These primary societies are like the ancient forests of our human history, with similar depths and diversities (and simultaneously "ancient" and "virgin"). The *lore* of wild nature is being lost along with the inhabitory human cultures. Each has its own humus of custom, myth, and lore that is now being swiftly lost—a tragedy for us all.

Brazil provides incentives for this kind of destructive development. Even as some mitigations are promised, there are policies in place that actively favor large corporations, displace natives, and at the same time do nothing for the mainstream poor. America disempowers Third World farmers by subsidizing overproduction at home. Capitalism plus big government often looks like welfare for the rich, providing breaks to companies that clearcut timber at a financial loss to the public. The largest single importer of tropical hardwoods is Japan (Mazda, Mitsubishi) and the second largest is the USA.

We must hammer on the capitalist economies to be at least capitalist enough to see to it that the corporations which buy timber off our public lands pay a fair market price for it. We must make the hard-boiled point that the world's trees are virtually worth more standing than they would be as lumber, because of such diverse results of deforestation as life-destroying flooding in Bangladesh and Thailand, the extinction of millions of species of animals and plants, and global warming. And, finally, we are not speaking only of forest-dwelling cultures or endangered species like voles or lemurs when we talk of ecological integrity and sustainability. We are looking at the future of our contemporary urban-industrial society as well. Not so long ago the forests were our depth, a sun-dappled underworld, an inexhaustible timeless source. Now they are vanishing. We are all endangered yokels. (*Yokel*: some English dialect, originally meaning "a green woodpecker or yellowhammer.")

On the Path,
Off the Trail

Work in Place of Place

Place is one kind of place. Another field is the work we do, our calling, our path in life. Membership in a place includes membership in a community. Membership in a work association—whether it's a guild or a union or a religious or mercantile order—is membership in a network. Networks cut across communities with their own kind of territoriality, analogous to the long migrations of geese and hawks.

Metaphors of path and trail are from the days when journeys were on foot or by horse with packstock, when our whole human world was a network of paths. There were paths everywhere: convenient, worn, clear, sometimes even set with distance posts or stones to measure *li*, or *versts*, or *yojana*. In the forested mountains north of Kyoto I came on mossy stone measuring posts almost lost in the dense bamboo-grass ground cover. They marked (I learned much later) the dried-herring-by-backpack trade route from the Japan Sea to the old capital. There are famous trails, the John Muir trail on the crest of the High Sierra, the Natchez Trace, the Silk Road.

A path is something that can be followed, it takes you somewhere. "Linear." What would a path stand against? "No path." Off the path, off the trail. So what's *off* the path? In a sense everything *else* is off the path. The relentless complexity of the world is off to the side of the trail. For hunters and herders trails weren't always so useful. For a forager, the path is *not* where you walk for long. Wild herbs, camas bulbs, quail, dye plants, are away from the path. The whole range of items that fulfill our needs is out there. We must wander through it to learn and memorize the field—rolling, crinkled, eroded, gullied, ridged (wrinkled like the brain)—holding the map in mind. This is the economic-visualization-meditation exercise of the Inupiaq and Athapaskans of Alaska of this very day. For the forager, the beaten path shows nothing new, and one may come home empty-handed.

In the imagery of that oldest of agrarian civilizations, China, the path or the road has been given a particularly strong place. From the earliest days of Chinese civilization, natural and practical processes have been described in the language of path or way. Such connections are explicit in the cryptic Chinese text that seems to have gathered all the earlier lore and restated it for later history—the *Dao De Jing*, "The Classic of the Way and the Power." The word *dao* itself means way, road, trail, or to lead/follow. Philosophically it means the nature and way of truth. (The terminology of Daoism was adopted by early Chinese Buddhist translators. To be either a Buddhist or Daoist was to be a "person of the way.") Another extension of the meaning of *dao* is the practice of an art or craft. In Japanese, *dao* is pronounced *dō*—as in *kadō*, "the way of flowers," *bushidō*, "way of the warrior," or *sadō*, "tea ceremony."

In all the traditional arts and crafts there has been customary apprenticeship. Boys or girls of fourteen or so were apprenticed to a potter, or a company of carpenters, or weavers, dyers, vernacular pharmacologists, metallurgists, cooks, and so forth. The youngsters left home to go and sleep in the back of the potting shed and would be given the single task of mixing clay for three years, say, or sharpening chisels for three years for the carpenters. It was often unpleasant. The apprentice had to submit to the idiosyncrasies and downright meanness of the teacher and not complain. It was understood that the teacher would test one's patience and fortitude endlessly. One could not think of turning back, but just take it, go deep, and have no other interests. For an apprentice there was just this one study. Then the apprentice was gradually inducted into some not so obvious moves, standards of craft, and in-house working secrets. They also began to experience—right then, at the beginning—what it was to be "one with your work." The student hopes not only to learn the mechanics of the trade but to absorb some of the teacher's power, the *mana*—a power that goes beyond any ordinary understanding or skill.

In the Zhuang-zi (Chuang-tzu) book, a third-century-B.C. witty radical Daoist text, perhaps a century or so after the *Dao De Jing*, there are a number of craft and "knack" passages:

> The Cook Ting cut up an ox for Lord Wenhui with dance-like grace and ease. "I go along with the natural makeup, strike in the big hollows, guide the knife through the big openings, and follow things as they are. So I never touch the smallest ligament or tendon, much less a main joint. . . . I've had this knife of mine for nineteen years and I've cut up thousands of oxen with it, and yet the blade is as good as though it had just come from the grindstone. There are spaces between the joints, and the blade of the knife has really no thickness. If you insert what has no thickness into such spaces, then there's plenty of room. . . . That's why after nineteen years the blade of my knife

is still as good as when it first came from the grindstone." "Excellent!" said Lord Wenhui. "I have heard the words of Cook Ting and learned how to care for life!"   Watson, 1968, 50–51

These stories not only bridge the spiritual and the practical, but also tease us with an image of how totally accomplished one might become if one gave one's whole life up to a work.

The occidental approach to the arts—since the rise of the bourgeoisie, if we like—is to downplay the aspect of accomplishment and push everyone to be continually doing something new. This puts a considerable burden on the workers of every generation, a double burden since they think they must dismiss the work of the generation before and then do something supposedly better and different. The emphasis on mastering the tools, on repetitive practice and training, has become very slight. In a society that follows tradition, creativity is understood as something that comes almost by accident, is unpredictable, and is a gift to certain individuals only. It cannot be programmed into the curriculum. It is better in small quantities. We should be grateful when it comes along, but don't count on it. Then when it *does* appear it's the real thing. It takes a powerful impulse for a student-apprentice who has been told for eight or ten years to "always do what was done before," as in the production tradition of folk pottery, to turn it a new way. What happens then? The old guys in this tradition look and say, "Ha! You did something new! Good for you!"

When the master artisans reach their mid-forties they begin to take on apprentices themselves and pass their skills along. They might also take up a few other interests (a little calligraphy on the side), go on pilgrimages, broaden themselves. If there is a next step (and strictly speaking there need not be one, for the skill of the accomplished craftsperson and the production of impeccable work that reflects the best of the tradition is certainly enough in one lifetime), it is to "go beyond training" for the final flower, which is not guaranteed by effort alone. There is a point beyond which training and practice cannot take you. Zeami, the superlative fourteenth-century Noh drama playwright and director who was also a Zen priest, spoke of this moment as "surprise." This is the surprise of discovering oneself needing no self, one with the work, moving in disciplined ease and grace. One knows what it is to *be* a spinning ball of clay, a curl of pure white wood off the edge of a chisel—or one of the many hands of Kannon the Bodhisattva of Compassion. At this point one can be free, with the work and from the work.

No matter how humble in social status, the skilled worker has dignity and pride—and his or her skills are needed and respected. This is not to be taken as any sort of justification for feudalism: it is simply a description of one side of how things worked in earlier times. The Far Eastern craft-and-training mystique eventually reached every corner of Japanese culture from noodle-making (the movie *Tampopo*) to big business to the high-culture arts. One of the vectors of this spread was Zen Buddhism.

Zen is the crispest example of the "self-help" (*jiriki*) wing of Mahayana Buddhism. Its community life and discipline is rather like an apprenticeship program in a traditional craft. The arts and crafts have long admired Zen training as a model of hard, clean, worthy schooling. I'll describe my experience as a *koji* (lay adept) at the monastery of Daitoku-ji, a Rinzai Zen sect temple in Kyoto, in the sixties. We sat cross-legged in meditation a minimum of five hours a day. In the breaks everyone did physical work—gardening, pickling, firewood cutting, cleaning the baths, taking turns in the kitchen. There were interviews with the teacher, Oda Sessō Rōshi, at least twice a day. At that moment we were expected to make a presentation of our grasp of the koan that had been assigned us.

We were expected to memorize certain sutras and conduct a number of small rituals. Daily life proceeded by an etiquette and a vocabulary that was truly archaic. A steady schedule of meditation and work was folded into weekly, monthly, and annual cycles of ceremonies and observations which went back to Song-dynasty China and in part clear back to the India of Shakyamuni's time. Sleep was short, the food was meager, the rooms spare and unheated, but this (in the sixties) was as true in the worker's or farmer's world as it was in the monastery.

(Novices were told to leave their pasts behind and to become one-pointed and unexceptional in all ways except the intention to enter this narrow gate of concentration on their koan. *Hone o oru*, as the saying goes—"break your bones," a phrase also used (in Japan) by workingmen, by the martial arts halls, and in modern sports and mountaineering.)

We also worked with lay supporters, often farmers, in downright convivial ways. We would stand out back in the vegetable gardens with locals discussing everything from new seed species to baseball to funerals. There were weekly begging walks down city streets and country lanes chanting and pacing along, our faces hidden under a big basket hat (waterproofed and dyed brown with persimmon juice). In fall the community made special begging trips for radishes or rice to country regions three or four ranges of hills away.

But for all its regularity, the monastic schedule could be broken for special events: on one occasion we all traveled by train to a gathering of hundreds of monks at a small but exquisite country temple for the celebration of its founding exactly five hundred years before. Our group came to be kitchen-workers: we labored for days chopping, cooking, washing, and arranging alongside the farm wives of the district. When the big feast was served we were the servers. That night, after the hundreds of guests had left, the kitchen-workers and laborers had their own feast and party, and old farmers and their wives traded crazy funny dances and songs with the Zen monks.

Freedom at Work

During one of the long meditation retreats called *sesshin*, the Rōshi lectured on the phrase "The perfect way is without difficulty. Strive hard!" This is the fundamental paradox of the way. One can be called on not to spare one's very bones in the intensity of effort, but at the same time we must be reminded that the path itself offers no hindrance, and there is a suggestion that the effort itself can lead one astray. Mere effort can heap up learning, or power, or formal accomplishment. Native abilities may be nourished by discipline, but discipline alone will not get one into the territory of "free and easy wandering" (a Zhuang-zi term). One must take care not to be victimized by one's penchant for self-discipline and hard work. One's lesser talents may lead to success in craft or business, but then one might never find out what one's more playful capacities might have been. "We study the self to forget the self," said Dōgen. "When you forget the self, you become one with the ten thousand things." Ten thousand things means all of the phenomenal world. When we are open that world can occupy us.

Yet we are still called on to wrestle with the curious phenomenon of the complex human self, needed but excessive, which resists letting the world in. Meditation practice gives us a way to scrape, soften, tan it. The intent of the koan theme is to provide the student with a brick to knock on the gate, to get through and beyond that first barrier. There are many further koans that work deeper into nondualistic seeing and being—enabling the student (as the tradition would like to have it) to ultimately be mindful, graceful, grateful, and skillful in daily life; to go beyond the dichotomy of natural and "worked." In a sense it's a practice of "an art of life."

The *Dao De Jing* itself gives us the most subtle interpretation of what the way might mean. It starts out by saying this: "The way that can be followed ('wayed') is not the constant way." *Dao ke dao fei chang dao*. First line, first chapter. It is saying: "A path that can be followed is not a *spiritual* path." The actuality of things cannot be confined within so linear an image as a road. The intention of training can only be accomplished when the "follower" has been forgotten. The way is without difficulty—it does not itself propose obstacles to us, it is open in all directions. We do, however, get in our own way—so the Old Teacher said "Strive hard!"

There are also teachers who say: "Don't try to prove something hard to yourself, it's a waste of time; your ego and intellect will be getting in your way; let all such fantastic aspirations go." They would say, at this very moment, just *be* the very mind that reads *this* word and effortlessly knows it—and you will have grasped the Great Matter. Such were the instructions of Ramana Maharshi, Krishnamurti, and the Zen Master Bankei. This was Alan Watts' version of Zen. One whole school of Buddhism takes this position—Jodo-shin, or Pure Land Buddhism, which elegant old Morimoto Roshi (who spoke Osaka dialect) said "is the only school of Buddhism that can scold Zen." It can scold it, he said, for trying too hard, for considering itself too special, and for being proud. One must have respect for the nakedness of these teachings and their ultimate correctness. Pure Land Buddhism is the purest. It resolutely resists any and all programs of self-improvement and stands only by *tariki*, which means "other-help." The "other" that might help is mythologically described as "Amida Buddha." Amida is no other than "emptiness"—the mind without conceptions or intentions, the Buddha-mind. In other words: "Give up trying to improve yourself, let the true self be yourself." These teachings are frustrating for motivated people in that no real instruction is offered the hapless seeker.

Then there have always been countless unacknowledged Bodhisattvas who did not go through any formal spiritual training or philosophical quest. They were seasoned and shaped in the confusion, suffering, injustice, promise, and contradictions of life. They are the unselfish, big-hearted, brave, compassionate, self-effacing, ordinary people who in fact have always held the human family together.

There are paths that can be followed, and there is a path that cannot—it is not a path, it is the wilderness. There is a "going" but no goer, no destination, only the whole field. I first stumbled a bit off the trail in the mountains of the Pacific Northwest, at twenty-two, while a fire lookout in the North Cascades. I then determined that I would study Zen in Japan. I had a glimpse of it again looking down the aisle of a library in a Zen temple at age thirty and it helped me realize that I should not live as a monk. I moved near the monastery and participated in the meditation, the ceremonies, and the farm-work as a layperson.

I returned to North America in 1969 with my then wife and first-born son and soon we moved to the Sierra Nevada. In addition to the work with farms, trees, and politics my neighbors and I have tried to keep up some formal Buddhist practice. We have deliberately kept it lay and nonprofessional. The Japanese Zen world of the last few centuries has become so expert and professional in the matter of strict training that it has lost to a great extent the capacity to surprise itself. The entirely dedicated and good-hearted Zen priests of Japan will defend their roles as specialists by pointing out that ordinary people cannot get into the finer points of the teachings because they cannot give enough time to it. This need not be the case for the lay-person, who can be as intent on his or her Buddhist practice as any worker, artisan, or artist would be with their work.

The structure of the original Buddhist order was inspired by the tribal governance of the Shakya ("Oak Tree") nation—a tiny repub-lic somewhat like the League of the Iroquois—with democratic rules of voting (Gard, 1949; 1956). Gautama the Buddha was born a Shakya—hence his appellation Shakyamuni, "sage of the Shak-yas." The Buddhist sangha is thus modeled on the political forms of a neolithic-derived community.

So our models for practice, training, and dedication need not be limited to monasteries or vocational training, but can also look to original communities with their traditions of work and sharing. There are additional insights that come only from the nonmonastic experience of work, family, loss, love, failure. And there are all the ecological-economical connections of humans with other living beings, which cannot be ignored for long, pushing us toward a pro-found consideration of planting and harvesting, breeding and slaughtering. All of us are apprenticed to the same teacher that the religious institutions originally worked with: reality.

Reality-insight says get a sense of immediate politics and history, get control of your own time; master the twenty-four hours. Do it well, without self-pity. It is as hard to get the children herded into the car pool and down the road to the bus as it is to chant sutras in the Buddha-hall on a cold morning. One move is not better than the other, each can be quite boring, and they both have the virtuous quality of repetition. Repetition and ritual and their good results come in many forms. Changing the filter, wiping noses, going to meetings, picking up around the house, washing dishes, checking the dipstick—don't let yourself think these are distracting you from your more serious pursuits. Such a round of chores is not a set of difficulties we hope to escape from so that we may do our "practice" which will put us on a "path"—it *is* our path. It can be its own fulfillment, too, for who would want to set enlightenment against nonenlightenment when each is its own full reality, its own complete delusion. Dōgen was fond of saying that "practice *is* the path." It's easier to understand this when we see that the "perfect way" is not a path that leads somewhere easily defined, to some goal that is at the end of a progression. Mountaineers climb peaks for the great view, the cooperation and comradeship, the lively hardship—but mostly because it *puts you out there* where the unknown happens, where you encounter surprise.

The truly experienced person, the refined person, *delights in the ordinary*. Such a person will find the tedious work around the house or office as full of challenge and play as any metaphor of mountaineering might suggest. I would say the real *play* is in the act of going totally off the trail—away from any trace of human or animal regularity aimed at some practical or spiritual purpose. One goes out onto the "trail that cannot be followed" which leads everywhere and nowhere, a limitless fabric of possibilities, elegant variations a millionfold on the same themes, yet each point unique. Every boulder on a talus slope is different, no two needles on a fir tree are identical. How could one part be more central, more important, than any other? One will never come onto the three-foot-high heaped-up nest of a Bushy-tailed Woodrat, made of twigs and stones and leaves, un-less one plunges into the manzanita thickets. Strive hard!

We find some ease and comfort in our house, by the hearth, and on the paths nearby. We find there too the tedium of chores and the staleness of repetitive trivial affairs. But the rule of impermanence means that nothing is repeated for long. The ephemerality of all our acts puts us into a kind of wilderness-in-time. We live within the nets of inorganic and biological processes that nourish everything, bumping down underground rivers or glinting as spiderwebs in the sky. Life and matter at play, chilly and rough, hairy and tasty. This is of a larger order than the little enclaves of provisional orderliness that we call ways. It *is* the Way.

Our skills and works are but tiny reflections of the wild world that is innately and loosely orderly. There is nothing like stepping away from the road and heading into a new part of the watershed. Not for the sake of newness, but for the sense of coming home to our whole terrain. "Off the trail" is another name for the Way, and sauntering off the trail is the practice of the wild. That is also where—paradox-ically—we do our best work. But we need paths and trails and will always be maintaining them. You first must be on the path, before you can turn and walk into the wild.

The Woman Who Married a Bear

The Story

Once there was a little girl, about ten years old. She used to go pick berries every summer. Every summer she would go with her family and they would pick berries and dry them. Sometimes they would see bear droppings on the trail. Girls had to be careful about bear droppings, they shouldn't walk over them. Men could walk over them, but young girls had to walk around them. But she loved to jump over the bear droppings, and kick them. She would disobey her mother. All the time she would see them and kick them and step over them. She kept seeing them all around her. She did this from childhood.

She grew up. One summer they were all going out to pick berries, dry fish, and camp. She was with her mother and aunts and sisters all day picking berries. It was toward the end of the day, and she saw some bear droppings. She said all kinds of words to them, kicked them, and jumped over them. The ladies were getting ready to go home, lifting up their burden baskets of blueberries. The young woman saw some extra-good berries and was picking them as the others went ahead. As she started to catch up she slipped, and spilled some of her berries on the ground. So she was bending over and picking them off the ground. The others went on down.

A man was standing there, dressed up fine, his face painted red. She saw him in the shadows. She had never seen him before. He said, "I know where there are lots of big berries, better than those. Let's go fill your basket. I'll walk you home." And they picked a while. It was getting dark. But he said, "There's another good place"—and soon it was dark. He said, "It's too late to go home. Let's fix a dinner." And he cooked over a fire, it looked like a fire. They ate some gopher. And then they made a bed in the leaves. When they went to bed he said, "Don't lift your head in the morning and look at me, even if you wake up before I do."

Next morning when they woke the young man said to her, "We can go on. We'll eat cold gopher. We won't make a fire. Let's get lots of berries." The young woman talked about going home, about her father and mother, and he said, "Don't be afraid. I'll go home with you." Then he slapped his hand down right on top of her head and put a circle around the woman's head with his finger, the way the sun goes. Then she forgot and didn't talk about home any more.

Then she forgot all about going home. She just went about with him, picking berries. Every time they camped it seemed like a month to her, but it was really only a day. They kept traveling from mountain to mountain. Finally she recognized a place. It looked like a place where she and her family used to go and dry meat. He stopped there at the timberline and slapped her head, and made a circle sunwise, and then another on the ground where she was sitting. He said, "Wait here. I am going hunting gophers. We have no meat. Wait till

I come back." Then he came back with the gophers. In the evening they made camp and cooked.

Next morning they got up and traveled on. At last she knew. It was getting near fall, and it was cold. She knew he was a bear. He said, "It's time to make a home" and started digging a den. She really knew he was a bear then. He got quite a ways digging the den and then he said, "Go get some fir boughs and some brush." She broke the branches from up high and brought him a bundle. He saw that and said, "Those limbs are no good. You left a mark and the people will see it and know we were here. We can't stay here." So they left.

They went up to the head of a valley. She recognized this valley. It was where her brothers used to go to hunt and eat bear. They would take the dogs there in April and hunt bear. They would send the dogs into the bear den, and then the bear would come out. That's where her brothers used to go. She knew it.

Her husband dug a den again and sent her out for brush. He said, "Get some brush that is lying on the ground—not from up high. No one will see where you got it, and it will become covered with snow." She did break it from low to the ground, but she also bent some high-up branches too. She let them hang down so her brothers would know. She rubbed sand on herself too—all over her body and limbs. And then she rubbed the trees around, so that the dogs would find her scent. Then she went to the den with her bundles of brush.

When the man was digging he looked like a bear. That was the *only* time. But the rest of the time he looked like a human being. The woman didn't know how else to stay alive, so she stayed with him as long as he was good to her.

"This is better," he said, and he carried the brush inside and fixed the den. After he fixed the den they left. The Grizzly Bear is the last to go into the den; they like to go around in the snow. So then he spent more days hunting gophers for the winter. She never saw him do it; she sat in the late autumn sun and looked down the valley. He didn't want her to see him digging up gophers like a grizzly bear.

Nearly every day he hunted gophers and they picked berries. He was just like a human to her.

It was really late in the fall. He said, "Well, I guess we'll go home now. We have enough food and berries. We'll go down." So they went into the den and stayed there and slept. They woke once a month and ate, and then went back to bed. Each month seemed like another morning, just like another day. They never really went outside, it just seemed like it.

Soon the woman found she was carrying a baby. And then in the middle of the winter, in the den, she had two little babies—one was a girl, and the other was a boy. She had them when the bears have their cubs.

Her husband used to sing in the night and she woke up to hear him. The bear became like a shaman when he started living with the woman. The song just came upon him, like a shaman. He sang it twice. She heard it the first time. The second time he made a sound, "Wuf! Wuf!" and she woke up.

"You're my wife, and I am going to leave soon. It looks like your brothers are going to come up here soon, before the snow is gone. I want you to know that I am going to do something bad. I am going to fight back!"

"Don't do it! They are your brothers-in-law! If you really love me you'll love them too. Don't kill them. Let them kill you! If you really love me don't fight! You have treated me well. Why did you live with me, if you are going to kill them?" "All right," he said. "I won't fight, but I want you to know what would happen!" His big canine teeth looked like swords. "These are what I fight with," he said. She kept pleading. "Don't do anything. I'll still have my children if they kill you!" She really knew he was a bear then.

They went back to sleep. When she woke again he was singing his song. "It's true," he said. "They are coming close. If they do kill me I want you to get my skull and my tail from them. Wherever they kill me build a big fire, and burn my head and tail and sing this song while the head is burning. Sing it until they are all burnt up!" And he sang the song again.

Then they ate some food and went back to bed. Another month went by. They didn't sleep well that month. He kept waking up. "It's coming close," he said. "I can't sleep well. It's getting to be bare ground. Look out and see if the snow is melted in front of the den." She looked out, and there was mud and sand. She grabbed some and made a ball and rubbed it over herself. It was full of her scent. She rolled it down the hill—then the dogs could smell it. She came in and said, "There is bare ground all over in some places." He asked her why she had made the marks. "Why? Why? Why? They'll find us easy!"

They slept for half a month, and then they woke. He was singing again. "This is the last one," he said. "You will not hear me again. Any time now the dogs will be at the door. They are close. Well, I'll fight back! I am going to do something bad!" His wife said, "You know they are my brothers! Don't do it! Who will look after my children if you kill them? You must think of the kids. My brothers will help me. If my brothers hunt you, let them be!" They went back to bed for just a little while. Next morning he said, "Well, it's close! It's close! Wake up!"

Just when they were getting up they heard a noise. "The dogs are barking. Well, I'll leave. Where are my knives? I want them!" He took them down. She saw him putting in his teeth. He was a big Grizzly Bear.

"Please don't fight. If you wanted me, why did you go this far? Just think of the kids. Don't hurt my brothers!" He said, "You won't see me again!" and went. At the entrance he growled, and slapped something back into the den. It was a pet dog, a little bear dog. When he threw the dog in, she grabbed it and shoved it back in the brush under the nest. She put the dog there to keep it. She sat on it and kept it there so it couldn't get out. She wanted to keep it for a reason.

For a long time there was no noise. She went out of the den. She heard her brothers below. They had already killed the bear. She felt bad, and she sat down. She found an arrow, and she picked it up. Then she fitted the little dog with a string around his back. She tied the arrow on the little dog and he ran to his masters. The boys were down there dressing out the bear. They knew the dog. They noticed the arrow and took it off.

"It's funny," they said. "No one in a bear den would tie this on!" They talked about it and decided to send the youngest brother up to the den. A younger brother could talk to his sister, but an older brother couldn't. The older brothers said to the young one, "We lost our sister a year ago. Something could have happened. A bear might have taken her away. You are the youngest, don't be afraid. There is nothing up there but her. You go and see if she is there. Find out!"

He went. She was sitting there crying. The boy came up. She cried when she saw him. She said, "You boys killed your brother-in-law! I went with him last summer. You killed him, but tell the others to save me the skull and the tail. Leave it there for me. When you get home, tell mother to sew a dress for me so I can go home. Sew a dress for the girl, and pants and a shirt for the boy, and moccasins. And tell her to come and see me." He went back down and told his brothers, "This is our sister. She wants us to save the bear's head and tail."

They did this and they went home. They told their mother. She got busy and sewed. She had a dress and moccasins and clothes for the children. The next day she went up there. The mother came to the place, and put clothing on the little kids. Then they went down to where the bear was killed. The boys had left a big fire. The woman burned the head and the tail, then she sang the song, until all was ashes.

Then they went back to her home, but she didn't go right in. She wasn't used to the human smell. She said, "Get the boys to build a camp. I can't come right into the house. It will be quite a while." She stayed there a long time. Toward fall she finally came and stayed with her mother. All winter the kids grew.

Next spring her brothers wanted her to act like a bear. They had killed a female bear that had cubs, one male and one female. They wanted their sister to put on the hide and act like a bear. They fixed little arrows. They pestered her to play with them, and they wanted her two little children to play too. She didn't want it. She told her mother, "I can't do it! Once I do it, I will turn into a bear. I'm half there already. Hair is already showing on my arms and legs—it's quite long." If she had stayed there with her bear husband another summer she would have turned into a bear. "If I put on the bear hide, I'll turn into one," she said.

But they kept telling her to play. Then the boys sneaked up one day and threw the bear hides over her and her little ones. She walked off on four legs! She shook herself just like a bear—it just happened! She was a Grizzly Bear. She couldn't do a thing. She had to fight against the arrows. She killed them all off, even her mother. She didn't kill her youngest brother, not him. She couldn't help it. Tears were running down her face.

Then she went on her own. She had her two little cubs with her. They walked up the slope and back into the mountains.

So a Grizzly Bear is partly human. Now people eat Black Bear meat, but they still don't eat Grizzly meat, because Grizzlies are half human.

On "The Woman Who Married a Bear"

Salmonberries, Crowberries, Nagoonberries, Cloudberries, High Bush Cranberries, Low Bush Cranberries, Thimbleberries, Raspberries, Soapberries, Blackberries, Serviceberries, Manzanita Berries, Red Huckleberries, Blueberries . . .

The salmonberries ripen early, and most of the others toward the end of summer. The berries' sheen, aroma, little spike of flavor, sweetness, all handed down from long ago. Who is it for? The berries call the birds and bears to eat. It's a gift, but there's also a return, for now the seed will be moved away. The little seeds buried in the sweet globules will go traveling in birds' craws, in raccoon bowels, across the rocks, over the river, through the air, to be left on other forest soils to sprout anew.

Picking berries takes patience. The bears draw over the shoots and delicately rake through the clusters with their claws. People make wooden rakes that look like bear-claws and gather them into a basket, or beat the bushes with a wooden spoon toward a winnowing basket held in the other hand. Some women are fast! Picking with all the fingers of both hands, never bruising the berries. When the berries are ripe people go out picking every day, and then dry or pickle them with sourdock for the winter. Eating them does no harm to the bush or the seed. Maybe this story starts with berries.

From long ago the Brown Bears, the Grizzlies (but we wouldn't speak of them directly by such blunt names), have come to the berry fields. They have been out ranging and feeding since spring, ranging dozens or hundreds of miles, often alone. When they gather to the best slopes for berries, there may be many bears picking berries close together, so they manage not to wrangle.

They eat all summer building fat for winter. If for some reason they don't put on enough weight by late fall, the mothers' bodies will abort the little fetus, since midwinter nursing might draw down her strength. After they are done with the soapberries and blueberries on the mountains they go to the streams and rivers for the fall-run salmon.

(Chinook or King, Sockeye or Red or Nerka, Pink or Humpbacked, Dog or Keta, Cherry or Masu, the salmon come into rivers from as far south as the Sacramento and go all the way around the North Pacific to Korea. At every river on the rim there are bears.)

For a long time only the bears and birds were at the berry thickets and the rivers. The humans arrived later. At first they all got along. There was always a bit of food to share. Small animals might be as powerful as big ones. Some, and a few humans, could change skins, change masks. From time to time they all would cross into the spirit world for a Big Time or a contest. The human beings in the original time weren't so bad. Later they seemed to drift away. They got busy with each other and were spending all the time among themselves. They quit coming to meetings, and got more and more stingy. They learned a lot of little stuff, and forgot where they came from.

Some animals started avoiding human beings. Others were concerned because they liked the human people and enjoyed being near them for their funny ways. Bears sort of cared. They still wanted to be seen by people, to surprise them sometimes, even to be caught or killed by them, so they might go inside the houses and hear their music. Maybe that's why bears leave droppings in the trails. It's a way to warn people that they're near and avoid scaring them. If bears or people get a fright, someone might get hurt. When people see scats they can study them and see how new they are, and check what's being eaten. If it's berries this week, you should know. Scats are a window into a bear's life: they show where she's been. Then when the people go to the mountain they can whistle and also mind their minds, because everybody knows what humans are thinking.

Young girls like to run and jump and sing. Some of them like to poke fun, but it's not usually mean. Jump-rope, they jump and sing—hopscotch, they jump and sing. Still, a girl or woman shouldn't jump over bear droppings, or any droppings really, and neither should men. It's fine to look at them and think about such signs, but it would be foolish to have opinions about them. But this girl always stepped over them and kept talking about it. Perhaps she was being naughty, but we also have to say that she was an exceptional little girl who somehow felt drawn to the wild place.

Drawn to the wild. Bears are so powerful and calm. At the same time, they are the closest of all animals to humans. Everybody says, "After you take a bear's coat off, it looks just like a human." And they act human: they fool, they teach their cubs (who are rowdy and curious), and they remember. They are confident. They will eat little trifles, or knock down a moose, with equal grace. Their claws are delicate and precise: they can pick up a nut between two tips. They make love for hours. They are grumpy after naps. They can lope a hundred miles overnight. They seem to be indestructible. They know what is happening, where to go, and how to get there. They are forgiving. They can become enraged, and when they fight it's as though they feel no pain. They have no enemies, no fears, they can be silly, and they are big-hearted. They are completely at home in the world. They like human beings, and they decided long ago to let the humans join them at the salmon-running rivers and the berryfields.

This girl must have known some of that, and in a way she was calling to the bears. Most people know that breaking rules is bad, and when they do it in a sneaky way they feel they're doing wrong. Some people break the rules because of muddy hearts and greed. Certain people are clear, and break the rules because they want to *know*. They also understand that there's a price to pay, and won't complain.

The rules are matters of manners that have to do with knowledge and power, with life and death, because they deal with taking life and with one's own eating and dying. Human beings, in their ignorance, are apt to give offense. There's a world behind the world we see that is the same world but more open, more transparent, without blocks. Like inside a big mind, the animals and humans all can talk, and those who pass through here get power to heal and help. They learn how to behave, and how not to give offense. To touch this world no matter how briefly is a help in life. People seek it, but the seeking isn't easy. Shapes are fluid here. For a bear, all the beings look like bears. For a human, they all look like humans. Each creature has its stories and its oddities—all the animals with their funny natures acting out different roles. "When dragons and fish see water as a palace, it is just like human beings seeing a palace. They do not think it flows. If an outsider tells them, 'What you see as a palace is running water,' the dragons and fish will be astonished, just as we are when we hear the words, 'Mountains flow' "—Dōgen. And sometimes those who have the power, or a reason, or are just curious, walk across the borderlines.

So this young woman was grown now, and was picking berries with her family. The bears knew she was there. When she happened to fall behind to pick up the berries she had spilled from her basket, a young man stepped forward from the shadows to introduce himself and help her out. He was in his finest clothing, dressed like one who was going visiting. He was a human to her. And so she entered the in-between world, not exactly human, not exactly animal, where rain might look like fire, and fire might be rain. And he put her more sharply, more solidly, into it, patting her on the head so she forgot. They went under the tangled windfalls, and when they came out they had passed beneath a range of mountains. Each day is a month, or years.

But she didn't entirely forget. We are always in both worlds, because they aren't really two. But even though she remembered that she had a family and a home behind her, it was not too strong a pull, because she was in love. He was a strong, handsome man, and he loved her too. They were in the most beautiful of mountains, in the grand golden weather of late summer, with ripe berries on every slope. Her young maiden dreams were fulfilled. If she has learned to love a bear, he has had to overcome his prejudice against humans, who are weak, light, unpredictable, smelly. So they join in passion and conversation. They live at timberline.

But winter comes. Bears put on weight and grow thick coats. If they are making a new den, they select a place on a slope, dig downward and then up, putting the chamber under a mat of alpine tree roots or under a great slab of rock. The entrance passageway may be three to ten feet long and the chamber eight or ten feet wide. And then the bears break off limbs: they bend them over one arm and break them off with the other and so they gather bedding and place it up in the den. With the den made, the Grizzlies walk around, still hunting, as long as the weather's mild. When snow comes down in earnest, right while it's falling hard, the bear goes into the den, and the falling snow will cover up its tracks.

In the den bears cease to drink or eat or urinate or defecate for four or five months. They are alert and can wake up fairly quickly. Their bodies somehow metabolize their own waste. Though losing fat they increase their lean body mass and conserve their bone volume as though they were awake and active. They dream. Perhaps their dreams are of the gatherings in the Inner Mountains where Bear as "Lord of the Mountain" hosts a great feast for all the other animals.

For the young woman, this is a time of flashing back and forth between selves. The landscape reenters her story: she recognizes a valley. She sees her lover, her husband, first as a bear digging the den, then as a human who sits and chats with her. She helps him gather Balsam Fir boughs for the den and cannot keep herself from leaving marks, leaving signs, for her brothers who will seek her. With annoyance, sadness, and a certain fatalism, he sees this, and without growing angry with her, simply moves on and digs a new den, where she still leaves her scent.

And so they go down into the den. She's not a bear yet, so they put up food for her need. She gives birth to babies in the winter just like bears do. And then it comes that they must grapple with their fates, with their task. He "became like a shaman when he started living with the woman." He was no ordinary bear to be able to change forms and accept humanity, but the power is still coming on him. Elder bears watching over him from afar? Knowing that powers would be needed? A shaman sings songs of power. He sang such a song. If he hadn't known before what was coming, he senses it now:

her brothers, and a battle. He could kill them certainly, and keep his wife and children, and move deeper into the mountains and be safe. That is a temptation: he flashes between realms with the huge grizzly canine teeth that are swords/teeth/swords/teeth to her eyes.

But having come this far into the human realm, he has obligated himself to human custom too, and there is a firm rule which says that brothers-in-law must never fight. The children's name passes down on the mother's side, and the children will be raised by her brothers more than by their father. If they could only accept him as a brother-in-law! That would be an ideal family unit, odd only in that half the unit would be bears (for she is changing into one) and the other half human! What a moment of utopian dream it must have been for him.

She is practical. She knows her brothers will never accept him, and she feels her children must be raised as human. But she loves her husband—not just the handsome human, the bear body. She is getting hairy herself. For several weeks they must live with these choices and the fate that approaches them. He sings in the night again: it is the song that must be sung when a bear has been hunted and killed. He gives the instructions to her: "Wherever they kill me build a big fire, and burn my head and tail and sing this song while the head is burning. Sing it until they are all burnt up!"

So that is the reason they came together: for him to pass this instruction from the bear realm to the human, via her. They both know it now. But he can't quite let it go—he says, "Why? Why?"—and even the final day there's one more thought of fighting back. She always stresses *brothers* and he can't go against that. Out the door he goes on the way to his death, knocking the little Tahltan bear dog behind him with a swipe of the paw. The pet dog is somewhere between wild animal and human, and helps prepare her to rejoin the human. Her husband dies out of sight, but she can hear the barking of the dogs. She sits and weeps, letting the loss and sorrow she was holding back come forth: she pours it out on her younger brother—"You

boys just killed your brother-in-law!" which is a grievous thing for
them, as well.

(Bears emerge from the den in the spring gaunt and hungry, and
fill up on Spring Beauties or such if they can't find a winter-killed elk
or moose or caribou carcass.)

She burns the head and tail and sings the song.

She cannot go back to her mother's house. She spends all summer
getting used to the human smell—and mourning. That fall and
winter, living in the village, she is teaching her relatives what she
learned—to burn the skull and tail of a bear after you kill it—and
she teaches them the song. There is much more that she learned from
her husband about the proper hunting and the ceremony of the bear,
and she teaches it all—to be indirect, not to boast, not to point at a
bear, to talk slow.

It's not an easy winter. The children don't fit in, nor does she.
People don't talk comfortably to her. The brothers are carrying dark
and difficult thoughts about their sister who knows so much about
bears. They set out the following spring on their annual bear-hunt
and come back with the pelt of a female and two cubs. They push,
push, their sister to play bear. Secrets not to be told are bothering
them: their sister, a bear. What did they eat? What did they speak
of? What does she dream? What was it like? How much power does
she have now, can she be trusted? What will her children become?
Her power and the mystery that surrounds her now go beyond what
is comfortable for the humans.

She tries to get her mother to stop them, knowing what will happen, her hair already growing longer. But it happens: the brothers
cannot stand this ambiguity: they push her over the line. She turns
back into a bear and kills them all except the younger brother. So
now they have paid for killing their brother-in-law, and paid for teas-
ing and pushing, and the mother has died too. The young woman
and her children are irrevocably bears now: the human world will not
accept them. They must return to the wilderness, having accom-

plished their task—to teach humans the precise manners in regard to bears. Perhaps all this was planned by the Bear Fathers and Mothers, who chose an intrepid young male to be the messenger. For each of the actors there was a price: the bear and the woman's family lost their lives. One cannot cross between realms without paying a high price. She lost her lover and her humanity to become a bear with two rowdy cubs alone in the wild.

That was very long ago. After that time human beings had good relations with the bears. Around the top of the world many peoples have hunted and celebrated and feasted with the bears outdoors in the snow every year in midwinter. Bears and people have shared the berryfields and the salmon streams without much trouble summer after summer. Bears have been careful not to hunt and kill humans as prey, although they would fight back when attacked.

Their story had further consequences: the bear wife was remembered by human beings as a goddess under many names, and there were many stories about her children and what they did in the world.

But that period is over now. The bears are being killed, the humans are everywhere, and the green world is being unraveled and shredded and burned by the spreading of a gray world that seems to have no end. If it weren't for a few old people from the time before, we wouldn't even know this tale.

Maria Johns and the Telling of This Story

This version of "The Woman Who Married a Bear" is based on a telling by Maria Johns to Catherine McClellan, an anthropologist and ethnohistorian. There are many versions of this story, and eleven of them are examined in McClellan's study *The Girl Who Married the Bear: A Masterpiece of Indian Oral Tradition* (1970). Of Maria Johns she wrote:

"Maria Johns was born probably some time in the 1880s. The first time she saw a white man was when she and her family challenged the coastal Chilkoot and crossed the Chilkoot Pass to trade at Wilson's store in Dyea. This was in the eighties, and Maria was a young woman. Maria belonged to the *tuq'wedi* or *decitan* sib, and she traced her ancestry ultimately to the coastal Tlingit town of Angoon. While her first language was the Tagish dialect of Athapascan, she also spoke a good deal of Tlingit, which became, in fact, the chief native language of Tagish. She had little command of English.

"Although she seems to have led a rather rich, full life, she was in poor health and partly blind during most of her adult days. When I met her in 1948 she was totally blind and spent most of her days in bed covered with a gopherskin robe. Maria composed at least three songs of her own and she evidently told a great many stories to her children, judging by the repertoires of her two grown daughters.

"Maria volunteered the bear story on the morning of July 16, 1948. I had visited her in her daughter Dora's house, and had been asking if there were any ritual observances for bears.

"Maria was obviously a good raconteur. She pantomimed frequently, changed her voice to indicate that different characters were speaking, and imitated the sounds of the dogs and bears. She hurried the tale a bit at the end for she was worried that I might miss the train taking me from Carcross.

"Dora Austin Wedge, the interpreter, had been to school, and she speaks excellent English. Dora's daughter, Annie, was the only other person present. She was much interested in the story, which she evidently had not heard before."

Arkadia

Brown Bear, *Ursus Arctos*.

Arktos, Greek for bear, in Latin called *urs*, in Sanskrit *rksha*, in Welsh *arth* (King Arthur)—the Sanskrit probably yields *Rakshasas*, night-wandering demons who roar and howl and eat corpses. The proto-proto root, D. Padwa suggests, is "Rrrrrr!"

The "arctic" is where the bears are.

Arkas was the son of Zeus and the Bear-goddess Callisto. He was supposedly progenitor of the Arkades, people of Arkadia, "Bear People." They were worshipers of Pan and Hermes and Artemis, lady of wild things, also associated with bears.

Arkadia: the inland upland plateaus and ranges of the central Peloponnesus, with seven-thousand-foot peaks along the northern edge. Originally it was pine-oak forest and grassland. The other Greeks thought of the Arkadians as an aboriginal population who had always been there, and in fact they remained a tough and independent people throughout Greek history. They were not affected by the Dorian invasions. They were gardeners, herders, and hunters. Urban Greeks and Romans took them as the model of a resilient vernacular subsistence culture that did not lose its connection with nature. In the early centuries A.D. deforestation and soil exhaustion reduced the population, and in the eighth century Slavic immigrants brought something of an end to the old culture. Some of the original Arkadians doubtless knew and told some version of the story of "The Woman Who Married a Bear."

At the Bear Dance

A grandmotherly woman in a print dress is speaking to a grizzled hard-worn elder in logger jeans and suspenders: "There are spirits in everything, right?" He nods. She smiles, "You don't look too convinced."

The old man is tall and powerful, though a bit stooped. He has curly steely-gray shoulder-length hair, pants half out of ten-inch ranch boots, heavy rough hands with a broken thumb. He says, "The old-time people didn't have all the right words we have now from science, so they just called the sun's rays 'spirits.' They called a

lot of things 'spirits.' It wasn't that they were dumb, but they called
these power-things and energy-things 'spirits.' "

A young Anglo is listening in. The woman is intense, clear-eyed,
good-humored, and continues her own exposition: "There are a lot
of things forgotten. I found a lot of it out. It's not for everybody, it's
for our people. We need to teach the young ones."

In the dusty dance area, a circle of children is being formed. Marvin Potts in old felt hat, denim work jacket and jeans, scuffed work
boots, is shaping them up, explaining gently. An eight-foot pole is
set up in the dance area, with a bear-pelt hanging from it. At the base
of the pole is a heap of freshly gathered, still-damp-from-rinsing,
sagebrush (artemisia) stems and leaves. Everyone is helping themselves to little bundles of it. A ways up the slope is a shade-shelter
with a handgame in progress, the constant rhythm of the drumming
on the logs, and the singing rising and falling.

The woman and the two men stand on and on in the hot sun, the
crowd washing around them, the older man's voice so soft we can
barely hear. The younger man listens and only occasionally questions.

"Science went up so high," the old one says, "that now it's beginning to come back down. We're climbing up with our old-ways
knowledge, pretty soon we'll meet science coming down." A young
native woman has joined the group, and the older woman is saying,
"Don't call me a Maidu or a Concow, I'm a Tai. That's our name for
ourselves." The old man turns back to her and says "What's a Tai?"
"That's what I am," she says, "but you don't know it."

"Well, I'm a Maidu just like you," he says. She laughs easily, says
"You're really a ————" and speaks a rich native word. "It means
Middle Mountain." He repeats the word easily; he clearly knows it:
"Yes, it means Middle Mountain. So that's what we were?" —"Yes,
your group. The white anthropologists gave us all the name Maidu."
—"OK," he says and he turns back to the younger man. "I'll go
dance now. Come see us some time. We have a lot of trouble keeping

people from robbing our graveyard." "What do you do?" the white man asks. "I work part time in a sawmill." And he departs, gathering three tiny grandchildren and leading them into the children's inner circle of the Bear dance.

Marie Potts is in her wheelchair by a standing pole adorned with strips of maple bark that dangle down around it. A portable PA system is now working and Frank begins to sing: "*Weda . . . weda . . . weda . . .*" There are two circles, an inner one of children and an outer ring of adults. Both begin to revolve. Slowly, going clockwise, people waving their little bundles of wormwood in rhythm. Young and old, lots of whites, lots of native people, lots of colors in between.

Pretty soon the Bear Itself comes forth, the great head held far forward, the thick black pelt covering the back. The two front legs are arms with canes. The lower body of the Bear is wearing cut-off white jeans with the seams half open. He moves well, truly bearlike, weaves in and out through the dancers, goes in circles between them, cutting through, going backwards. He takes a child and leads it along with him under the bearskin, and then turns the child free. A little one bursts into tears as he comes near, while a small boy behind him whops his back with artemisia. He runs up at women, bothers them, they squeal and slap the artemisia at him. At times the song stops for a moment, and the singer gets a few breaths. The Bear goes over to Marie in her wheelchair, puts his paw around her shoulder, and nuzzles her. Her eyes glisten, her smile is intense and delighted.

Marvin meanwhile leads the circle of dancers, holding the maple-bark streamer pole aloft. (He had said that the twisted curls of bark are to be rattlesnake rattles, and that we play with Rattlesnake and Bear and give them good spirit and humor, so that we'll all get along through the summer.)

The round dance continues in its stately revolutions. Finally Marvin leads the circle out and away from the dance ground. The line of dancers, native men and women, children, middle-aged white ranchers in wranglers and resistols, weaves through the densely parked cars and pickups. It goes down between the cinnamon-brown trunks of shady Jeffrey Pines and around the handgame ramada (songs still going strong side by side with the music of the Bear dance), and then over a grassy slope to a fast-running stream where everyone spreads out along the banks and washes their hands and face with cool water. They let their bundles of artemisia float free with the creek. The bundles will flow through the pine forest, back down to the sagebrush, and disappear into the Great Basin.

This is the end of the Bear dance. The bearskin is hung up on the pole again, the people drift toward the whole-steer barbecue pit and the salmon that was a gift from some people on the coast. The power songs of the handgame players continue without break.

At Wepamkun, in Notokkoyo, Shasta, June of 40077

Survival and

Sacrament

> One time when the Master was washing his
> bowls, he saw two birds contending over a frog.
> A monk who also saw this asked, "Why does it
> come to that?"
>
> The Master replied, "It's only for your benefit."
>
> DONG-SHAN

An End to Birth

In the midst of the An Lushan rebellion and the destruction of
Ch'ang-an, the capital, Du Fu wrote a poem, "Spring View," that
grieves for Ch'ang-an and all of China. It opens:

> The State is destroyed, but the mountains and rivers survive.

It is one of the most famous of Chinese poems, well known in Japan
as well. The Japanese poet Nanao Sakaki has recently reversed this
line to give it a contemporary reading:

> The mountains and rivers are destroyed, but the State survives.

One has to travel outside North America to appreciate this. Speaking to a group of Chinese writers and intellectuals in Beijing in 1984

about the need to include riverbanks and forest slopes in the workers-and-peasants councils, I quoted Nanao's version of the great line. They responded with a pained laugh.

It is said that about a million and a half species of animals and plants have been scientifically described, and that there are anywhere from ten to thirty million species of organisms on earth. Over half of all the species on earth are thought to live in the moist tropical forests (Wilson, 1989, 108). About half of those forests, in Asia, Africa, and South America, are already gone. (At the same time there are seven million homeless children on the streets of Brazil. Are vanishing trees being reborn as unwanted children?) It looks like the remainder of the forests will be gone but for tiny patches by the year 2000. A clearcut or even a mile-wide strip-mine pit will heal in geological time. The extinction of a species, each one a pilgrim of four billion years of evolution, is an irreversible loss. The ending of the lines of so many creatures with whom we have traveled this far is an occasion of profound sorrow and grief. Death can be accepted and to some degree transformed. But the loss of lineages and all their future young is not something to accept. It must be rigorously and intelligently resisted.

Defend all of these plants, bugs, and animals equally? Little invertebrates that have never been seen in a zoo or a wildlife magazine? Species that are but a hair away from one another? It isn't just a case of unique lineages but the lives of overall ecosystems (a larger sort of almost-organism) that are at stake. Some archly argue that extinction has always been the fate of species and communities alike. Some quote a Buddhist teaching back at us: "all is impermanent." Indeed. All the more reason to move gently and cause less harm. Large highly adapted vertebrates, once lost, will never return in the forms we have known them. Hundreds of millions of years might elapse before the equivalent of a whale or an elephant is seen again, if ever. The scale of loss is beyond any measure the planet has ever known. "Death is one thing, an end to *birth* is something else" (Soule and Wilcox, 1980, 8).

But there is no end in view to birth for humans. The world's human population has doubled since mid-century to over five billion. It will be eight and a half billion by 2025. An estimated billion and a half people in the Third World will soon be running short of firewood, while people of the developed nations are driving five hundred million cars (Keyfitz, 1989, 121). Throughout the 1980s population growth outstripped economic growth in the Third World. There is no "demographic transition" visible on the horizon that will stabilize birthrates in the Third World.

There are criteria for discussing the carrying capacity of the planet. Proposing an ecologically optimal number of humans is not an automatic demand that some be killed or that abortion become mandatory, as some people seem to think. It is a proposal for discussion. If acted on, the reduction of numbers would be accomplished by a lower birthrate over decades or even centuries. I once speculated that 10 percent of the world's current (1990) population of five plus billion might be a target to aim for, one that would guarantee space and habitat for all, including wildlife. My figure has been quoted with a certain disbelief—citing my "obsession with wilderness" (Guha, 1989, 73). Population was 10 percent of what it is now about the year 1650! At that time the 550 million or so souls on earth were living in the presence of great architecture, art, and literature and debating long-established philosophies and religions—the same ones we still are grappling with.

Our immediate business, and our quarrel, is with ourselves. It would be presumptuous to think that Gaia much needs our prayers or healing vibes. Human beings themselves are at risk—not just on some survival-of-civilization level but more basically on the level of heart and soul. We are in danger of losing our souls. We are ignorant of our own nature and confused about what it means to be a human being. Much of this book has been the reimagining of what we have been and done, and the robust wisdom of our earlier ways. Like Ursula Le Guin's *Always Coming Home*—a genuine teaching text—this book has been a meditation on what it means to be human.

It is this present time, the twelve thousand or so years since the ice age and the twelve thousand or so years yet to come, that is our little territory. We will be judged or judge ourselves by how we have lived with each other and the world during these two decamillennia. If we are here for any good purpose at all (other than collating texts, running rivers, and learning the stars), I suspect it is to entertain the rest of nature. A gang of sexy primate clowns. All the little critters creep in close to listen when human beings are in a good mood and willing to play some tunes.

Cultured or Crabbed

We still only know what we know: "The flavors of the peach and the apricot are not lost from generation to generation. Neither are they transmitted by book-learning" (Ezra Pound). The rest is hearsay. There is strength, freedom, sustainability, and pride in being a practiced dweller in your own surroundings, knowing what you know. There are two kinds of knowing.

One is that which grounds and places you in your actual condition. You know north from south, pine from fir, in which direction the new moon might be found, where the water comes from, where the garbage goes, how to shake hands, how to sharpen a knife, how the interest rates work. This sort of knowledge itself can enhance public life and save endangered species. We learn it by revivifying culture, which is like reinhabitation: moving back into a terrain that has been abused and half-forgotten—and then replanting trees, dechannelizing streambeds, breaking up asphalt. What—some would say—if there's no "culture" left? There always is—just as much as there's always (no matter where) place and language. One's culture is in the family and the community, and it lights up when you start to do some real work together, or play, tell stories, act up—or when someone gets sick, or dies, or is born—or at a gathering like Thanksgiving. A culture is a network of neighborhoods or communities that is rooted and tended. It has limits, it is ordinary. "She's very cultured" shouldn't mean elite, but more like "well-fertilized."

(The term *culture* goes back to Latin meanings, via *colere*, such as "worship, attend to, cultivate, respect, till, take care of." The root *kwel basically means to revolve around a center—cognate with *wheel* and Greek *telos*, "completion of a cycle," hence *teleology*. In Sanskrit this is *chakra*, "wheel," or "great wheel of the universe." The modern Hindi word is *charkha*, "spinning wheel"—with which Gandhi meditated the freedom of India while in prison.)

The other kind of knowledge comes from straying outside. Thoreau writes of the crab apple, "*Our* wild apple is wild only like myself, perchance, who belong not to the aboriginal race here, but have strayed into the woods from cultivated stock." John Muir carries these thoughts along. In *Wild Wool* he quotes a farmer friend who tells him, "Culture is an orchard apple; Nature is a crab." (To go back to the wild is to become sour, astringent, crabbed. Unfertilized, unpruned, tough, resilient, and every spring *shockingly* beautiful in bloom.) Virtually all contemporary people are cultivated stock, but we can stray back into the woods.

One departs the home to embark on a quest into an archetypal wilderness that is dangerous, threatening, and full of beasts and hostile aliens. This sort of encounter with the other—both the inner and the outer—requires giving up comfort and safety, accepting cold and hunger, and being willing to eat anything. You may never see home again. Loneliness is your bread. Your bones may turn up someday in some riverbank mud. It grants freedom, expansion, and release. Untied. Unstuck. Crazy for a while. It breaks taboo, it verges on transgression, it teaches humility. Going out—fasting—

singing alone—talking across the species boundaries—praying—giving thanks—coming back.

On the mythical plane this is the source of the worldwide hero narratives. On the spiritual plane it requires embracing the other as oneself and stepping across the line—not "becoming one" or mixing things up but holding the sameness and difference delicately in mind. It can mean seeing the houses, roads, and people of your old place as for the first time. It can mean every word heard is heard to its deepest echo. It can mean mysterious tears of gratitude. Our "soul" is our dream of the other.

There is a movement toward creating a "culture of the wilderness" from within contemporary civilization. The Deep Ecology philosophers and the struggles and arguments which have taken place between them and the Green movement, the Social Ecologists, and the Ecofeminists are all part of the emerging realization that this could be tried. Deep Ecology thinkers insist that the natural world has value in its own right, that the health of natural systems should be our first concern, and that this best serves the interests of humans as well. They are well aware that primary people everywhere are our teachers in these values (Sessions and Devall, 1985). The emergence of Earth First! brings a new level of urgency, boldness, and humor into environmentalism. Direct-action techniques that go back to the civil rights and labor movement days are employed in ecological issues. With Earth First!, the Great Basin finally steps onto the stage of world politics. The established environmental organizations are forced by these mavericks to become more activist. At the same time there is a rapidly growing grassroots movement in Asia, Borneo, Brazil, Siberia. It is a cause for hope that so many people worldwide—from Czech intellectuals to rainforest-dwelling mothers in Sarawak—are awakening to their power.

The original American environmental tradition came out of the politics of public lands and wildlife (geese, fish, ducks—hence the

Audubon Society, the Izaak Walton League, and Ducks Unlimited). For decades a narrow but essential agenda of wilderness preservation took up everyone's volunteer time. With the 1970s "conservation" became "environmentalism" as concerns extended out of the wilderness areas to broader matters of forest management, agriculture, water and air pollution, nuclear power, and all the other issues we know so well.

Environmental concerns and politics have spread worldwide. In some countries the focus is almost entirely on human health and welfare issues. It is proper that the range of the movement should run from wildlife to urban health. But there can be no health for humans and cities that bypasses the rest of nature. A properly radical environmentalist position is in no way anti-human. We grasp the pain of the human condition in its full complexity, and add the awareness of how desperately endangered certain key species and habitats have become. We get a lot of our information—paradoxically—from deep inside civilization, from the biological and social sciences. The critical argument now within environmental circles is between those who operate from a human-centered resource management mentality and those whose values reflect an awareness of the integrity of the whole of nature. The latter position, that of Deep Ecology, is politically livelier, more courageous, more convivial, riskier, and more scientific.

It comes again to an understanding of the subtle but critical difference of meaning between the terms *nature* and *wild*. Nature is the subject, they say, of science. Nature can be deeply probed, as in microbiology. The wild is not to be made subject or object in this manner; to be approached it must be admitted from within, as a quality intrinsic to who we are. Nature is ultimately in no way endangered; wilderness is. The wild is indestructible, but we might not *see* the wild.

A culture of wilderness starts somewhere in this terrain. Civili-

zation is part of nature—our egos play in the fields of the unconscious—history takes place in the Holocene—human culture is
rooted in the primitive and the paleolithic—our body is a vertebrate
mammal being—and our souls are out in the wilderness.

> All together elsewhere, vast
> Herds of reindeer move across
> Miles and miles of golden moss,
> Silently and very fast.
>> W. H. Auden,
>> from "The Fall of Rome"

Grace

There is a verse chanted by Zen Buddhists called the "Four Great
Vows." The first line goes: "Sentient beings are numberless, I vow to
save them." *Shujō muhen seigando*. It's a bit daunting to announce this
intention—aloud—to the universe daily. This vow stalked me for
several years and finally pounced: I realized that I had vowed to let the
sentient beings save *me*. In a similar way, the precept against taking
life, against causing harm, doesn't stop in the negative. It is urging
us to *give* life, to *undo* harm.

Those who attain some ultimate understanding of these things
are called "Buddhas," which means "awakened ones." The word is
connected to the English verb "to bud." I once wrote a little parable:

Who the Buddhas Are

All the beings of the universe are already realized. That is, with the
exception of one or two beings. In those rare cases the cities, villages,
meadows, and forests, with all their birds, flowers, animals, rivers,
trees, and humans, that surround such a person, all collaborate to ed-
ucate, serve, challenge, and instruct such a one, until that person
also becomes a New Beginner Enlightened Being. Recently realized
beings are enthusiastic to teach and train and start schools and practices. Being able to do this develops their confidence and insight up

to the point that they are fully ready to join the seamless world of interdependent play. Such new enlightened beginners are called "Buddhas" and they like to say things like "I am enlightened together with the whole universe" and so forth. *Boat in a Storm*, 1987

Good luck! One might say. The test of the pudding is in the *eating*. It narrows down to a look at the conduct that is entwined with food. At mealtime (seated on the floor in lines) the Zen monks chant:

> Porridge is effective in ten ways
> To aid the student of Zen
> No limit to the good result
> Consummating eternal happiness

and

> Oh, all you demons and spirits
> We now offer this food to you
> May all of you everywhere
> Share it with us together

and

> We wash our bowls in this water
> It has the flavor of ambrosial dew
> We offer it to all demons and spirits
> May all be filled and satisfied
> *Om makula sai svaha*

And several other verses. These superstitious-sounding old ritual formulas are never mentioned in lectures, but they are at the heart of the teaching. Their import is older than Buddhism or any of the world religions. They are part of the first and last practice of the wild: *Grace*.

Everyone who ever lived took the lives of other animals, pulled plants, plucked fruit, and ate. Primary people have had their own ways of trying to understand the precept of nonharming. They knew that taking life required gratitude and care. There is no death that is not somebody's food, no life that is not somebody's death. Some would take this as a sign that the universe is fundamentally flawed. This leads to a disgust with self, with humanity, and with nature. Otherworldly philosophies end up doing more damage to the planet (and human psyches) than the pain and suffering that is in the existential conditions they seek to transcend.

The archaic religion is to kill god and eat him. Or her. The shimmering food-chain, the food-web, is the scary, beautiful condition of the biosphere. Subsistence people live without excuses. The blood is on your own hands as you divide the liver from the gallbladder. You have watched the color fade on the glimmer of the trout. A subsistence economy is a sacramental economy because it has faced up to one of the critical problems of life and death: the taking of life for food. Contemporary people do not need to hunt, many cannot even afford meat, and in the developed world the variety of foods available to us makes the avoidance of meat an easy choice. Forests in the tropics are cut to make pasture to raise beef for the American market. Our distance from the source of our food enables us to be superficially more comfortable, and distinctly more ignorant.

Eating is a sacrament. The grace we say clears our hearts and guides the children and welcomes the guest, all at the same time. We look at eggs, apples, and stew. They are evidence of plenitude, excess, a great reproductive exuberance. Millions of grains of grass-seed that will become rice or flour, millions of codfish fry that will never, and *must* never, grow to maturity. Innumerable little seeds are sacrifices to the food-chain. A parsnip in the ground is a marvel of living chemistry, making sugars and flavors from earth, air, water. And if we do eat meat it is the life, the bounce, the swish, of a great alert being with keen ears and lovely eyes, with foursquare feet and a huge beating heart that we eat, let us not deceive ourselves.

We too will be offerings—we are all edible. And if we are not devoured quickly, we are big enough (like the old down trees) to provide a long slow meal to the smaller critters. Whale carcasses that sink several miles deep in the ocean feed organisms in the dark for fifteen years. (It seems to take about two thousand to exhaust the nutrients in a high civilization.)

At our house we say a Buddhist grace—

> We venerate the Three Treasures [teachers, the wild, and friends]
> And are thankful for this meal
> The work of many people
> And the sharing of other forms of life.

Anyone can use a grace from their own tradition (and really give it meaning)—or make up their own. Saying some sort of grace is never inappropriate, and speeches and announcements can be tacked onto it. It is a plain, ordinary, old-fashioned little thing to do that connects us with all our ancestors.

> A monk asked Dong-shan: "Is there a practice for people to follow?"
> Dong-shan answered: "When you become a real person, there is such a practice."

Sarvamangalam, Good Luck to All.

Bibliography

Berg, Peter, and others. *A Green City Program for San Francisco Bay Area Cities and Towns*. San Francisco: Planet Drum, 1989.

Blainey, Geoffrey. *The Triumph of the Nomads*. Melbourne: Sun Books, 1976.

Cafard, Max. "The Surre(gion)alist Manifesto." *Mesechabe*, Autumn 1989.

Cook, Francis. *How to Raise an Ox*. Los Angeles: Center, 1979.

Cox, Susan Jane Buck. "No Tragedy in the Commons." *Environmental Ethics*, Spring 1985.

Dodge, Jim. "Living by Life." *CoEvolution Quarterly*, Winter 1981.

Dōgen. *Moon in a Dewdrop: Writings of Zen Master Dōgen*. Tanahashi, Kazuaki (trans.). San Francisco: North Point, 1985.

Dong-shan. *The Record of Tung-shan*. William F. Powell, trans. Honolulu: University of Hawaii Press, 1986.

Ferguson, Denzel, and Nancy Ferguson. *Sacred Cows at the Public Trough*. Bend, Ore.: Maverick, 1983.

Friedrich, Paul. *Proto-Indo-European Trees*. Chicago: University of Chicago Press, 1970.

Gard, Richard. *Buddhist Influences on the Political Thought and Institutions of India and Japan*. Phoenix Papers, no. 1. Claremont, 1949.

————. *Buddhist Political Thought*. Bangkok: Mahamukta University, 1956.

Gernet, Jacques. *Daily Life in China: On the Eve of the Mongol Invasion*. Stanford: Stanford University Press, 1962.

Grapard, Allan. "Flying Mountains and Walkers of Emptiness: Toward a Definition of Sacred Space in Japanese Religions." *History of Religions*, February 1982.

Guha, Ramachandra. "Radical Environmentalism and Wilderness Preservation: A Third World Critique." *Environmental Ethics*, Spring 1989.

Gumperz, John J. "Speech Variation and the Study of Indian Civilization." In Dell Hymes (ed.), *Language in Culture and Society*. New York: Harper & Row, 1964.

Hardin, Garrett, and John Baden. *Managing the Commons*. San Francisco: W. H. Freeman, 1977.

Hillman, James. *Blue Fire*. New York: Harper & Row, 1989.

Illich, Ivan. *Shadow Work*. London: Marion Boyars, 1981.

Jackson, Wes. *New Roots for Agriculture*. San Francisco: Friends of the Earth, 1980.
———. *Altars of Unhewn Stone: Science and the Earth*. San Francisco: North Point, 1987.

Kari, James. *Dena'ina Elnena, Tanaina Country*. Fairbanks: University of Alaska Native Languages Center, 1982.
———. *Native Place Names in Alaska: Trends in Policy and Research*. Montreal: McGill University Symposium on Indigenous Names in the North, 1985.

Keyfitz, Nathan. "The Growing Human Population." *Scientific American*, September 1989.

Kodera, Takashi James. *Dogen's Formative Years in China*. Boulder: Prajna Press, 1980.

Kroeber, A. L. *Cultural and Natural Areas of Native North America*. Berkeley: University of California Press, 1947.

Le Guin, Ursula K. *Always Coming Home*. New York: Harper & Row, 1985.

Maser, Chris. *The Redesigned Forest*. San Pedro, Calif.: R. & J. Miles, 1988.
———. *Primeval Forest*. San Francisco: Sierra Club, 1989.

McCay, Bonnie M., and James M. Acheson (eds.). *The Question of the Commons: The Culture and Ecology of Communal Resources*. Tucson: University of Arizona Press, 1987.

McClellan, Catherine. *The Girl Who Married the Bear: A Masterpiece of Indian Oral Tradition*. Publications on Ethnology, no. 2. Ottawa: Museum of Man, 1970.
———. *My Old People Say: An Ethnographic Survey of Southern Yukon Territory*. Pts. 1 and 2. Ottawa: Museum of Man, 1975.

Mitchell, John H. *Ceremonial Time*. New York: Doubleday, 1984.

Moyle, Peter, and F. Ranil Senanayake. "Wildlife Conservation in Sri Lanka: A Buddhist Dilemma." *Tigerpaper* 9, 1983.

Muir, John. "Wild Wool." In *Wilderness Essays*. Salt Lake City: Peregrine Smith, 1984.

Myers, Norman. *The Primary Source*. New York: Norton, 1984.

Netting, R. "What Alpine Peasants Have in Common: Observations on Communal Tenure in a Swiss Village." *Human Ecology*, 1976.

Polanyi, Karl. *The Great Transformation*. New York: Octagon Books, 1975.

Raise the Stakes. Journal of the Planet Drum Foundation. P.O. Box 31251, San Francisco, Calif. 94131.

Richards, John F., and Richard P. Tucker. *World Deforestation in the Twentieth Century*. Durham, N.C.: Duke University Press, 1988.

Robinson, Gordon. *The Forest and the Trees: A Guide to Excellent Forestry*. Covelo, Calif.: Island Press, 1988.

Sessions, George, and Bill Devall. *Deep Ecology*. Salt Lake City: Peregrine Smith, 1985.

Snyder, Gary. *Myths and Texts*. New York: New Directions, 1960.

———. *Turtle Island*. New York: New Directions, 1974.

———. *The Old Ways*. San Francisco: City Lights, 1977.

———. " 'Wild' in China." *CoEvolution Quarterly*, Fall 1978.

———. *He Who Hunted Birds in His Father's Village*. San Francisco: Gray Fox, 1979.

———. "Ink and Charcoal." *CoEvolution Quarterly*, Winter 1981.

Soule, Michael, and Bruce A. Wilcox (eds.). *Conservation Biology*. Sunderland, Mass.: Sinauer, 1980.

Thirgood, J. V. *Man and the Mediterranean Forest: A History of Resource Depletion*. New York: Academic Press, 1981.

Thoreau, Henry David. "Wild Apples." In *The Natural History Essays*. Salt Lake City: Peregrine Smith, 1984.

Todorov, Tzvetan. *The Conquest of America*. New York: Harper & Row, 1985.

Waring, R. H., and Jerry Franklin. "Evergreen Coniferous Forests of the Pacific Northwest." *Science*, 29 June 1979.

Watson, Burton (trans.). *The Complete Works of Chuang Tzu*. New York: Columbia University Press, 1968.

——. *Chinese Lyricism: Shih Poetry from the Second to the Twelfth Century*. New York: Columbia University Press, 1971.

Wilson, E. O. "Threats to Biodiversity." *Scientific American*, September 1989.

Zeami. *Kadensho*. Sakurai and others, trans. Kyoto: Doshisha University, 1968.

Design by David Bullen
Typeset in Mergenthaler Garamond #3
with Zapf International display
by Wilsted & Taylor
Printed by Maple-Vail
on acid-free paper